THE CROSSES OF LENT

SERMON BOOK

Sermons and Sermonic Studies

Dale A. Meyer and Hubert F. Beck

Publishing House
St. Louis

Copyright © 1987 Concordia Publishing House
3558 S. Jefferson Avenue, St. Louis, MO 63118-3968
Manufactured in the United States of America

Library of Congress Cataloging in Publication Data

Beck, Hubert E.
    The crosses of Lent.

    1. Lenten sermons. 2. Lent—Prayer-books and devotions—English. 3. Sermons, American. I. Meyer, Dale A., 1947–   . II. Title.
BV4277.B42   1987   252'.62   87-11721
ISBN 0-570-04478-2

1 2 3 4 5 6 7 8 9 10 WP 96 95 94 93 92 91 90 89 88 87

Contents

Foreword

"If we are not talking about the cross of Jesus Christ, we are off the subject." That maxim for all preaching is especially true for the season of Lent. Yet the preacher who tries, like St. Paul, to know nothing among his congregation but Jesus Christ, the Crucified, may find little time in the burdensome schedule of Lent to mine the depths and riches of "the wondrous cross."

The Crosses of Lent provides an integrated program to help both pastor and congregation explore the themes suggested by nine classic depictions of the cross. Sermon studies, outlines, and developed sermons are coordinated with banner designs as well as patterns for crosses to be distributed to the entire congregation. The history of each of The Crosses of Lent—the crosses of prophecy, humility, and hope, of suffering and regeneration, of mission and eternity—points us to an aspect of the rich meaning of the cross of Jesus.

Finally, of course, The Crosses of Lent culminate with the Passion Cross of the death of our Redeemer and the Cross of Glory, which is the cross seen from the vindication and triumph of Easter. The depths and riches of the cross include not only solemnity but also exaltation. The pastor and congregation who spend time in devotion and meditation on the cross in all its aspects will find, with the hymn writer, that "Sweet the moments rich in blessing, Which before the CROSS we spend."

Ash Wednesday

Tau Cross—Prophecy

Sermon Study

Text: John 3:14–15
Passion Reading: Matthew 26:1–13

Introduction

It is strange that seasons like Lent and Christmas, times that offer the richest worship experiences of the year, are the most burdensome to the pastor. One result is that the pastor does not schedule time to relax and ponder the spiritual importance of the season. When his spiritual batteries are run down, his parishioners may receive less than the best quality in their worship experiences. The words of the season end up being routine, the same words we've spoken and heard in this season for so many years. They barely touch the heart and have little effect on the life.

Jesus knew about words that don't sink in. More than once He had told the disciples that He was going to die and rise again, a prophecy you would have expected them to remember. Both the Passion reading and the sermon text for your first midweek service are instances of Jesus prophesying his crucifixion. In the passion reading He spells out the details not long before the climax of Holy Week. The sermon text came earlier in His ministry. It is that portion of Jesus' conversation with Nicodemus in which He uses the bronze serpent of Numbers 21 as a type of His own death. These and other predictions of the Passion should have been remembered by the disciples. They were remembered, but only after the events had taken place. Prophecy is like that. God's workings are best understood after the fact.

The Tau Cross is the cross of prophecy. It is said to be the shape of the cross that Moses used when he raised the bronze serpent. The Israelites are said to have drawn the Tau Cross in blood over their doorposts on Passover night. As the focal point of this week's worship, it gives us the opportunity to look back into Biblical history and see how God kept His promises. How wonderful! Since He fulfilled His prophecies about death and resurrection, He certainly will keep all His other promises to us. Lent can be a time of spiritual blessings—even for you, busy pastor. Let it be!

Background: The Cross

Whatever its shape (and you'll discover that the crosses in this series were designed by both artists and executioners!), the cross may not have a significant place in theologies of glory, but it is the place for which Jesus tried to prepare his disciples. And they didn't like it. Jews were appalled by the cross for various reasons.

It was a place of terrible torture. Originally, it was used by the Romans to humiliate public enemies. A person was fastened to a cross to be viewed and mocked by passersby but was later removed and continued to live. The cross's potential for torture was soon recognized, however, and it became the Roman instrument to execute foreigners. Without any body support, the crucified person died in a few hours from asphyxiation and muscle spasms. Supports for the feet or the buttocks of the victim became common because they could prolong the agony for days. But these agonies were not the greatest offense to Jesus' contemporaries, who, we must remember, were quite ready to resort to the inhumane method of stoning (Acts 6).

The greatest offense of the cross was nationalistic. Commonly used by the Phoenicians, Assyrians, and Persians, the Hebrews were taught that it was a curse on the Promised Land: "If a man guilty of a capital offense is put to death and his body is hung on a tree, you must not leave his body on the tree overnight. Be sure to bury him that same day, because anyone who is hung on a tree is under God's curse. You must not desecrate the land the Lord your God is giving you as an inheritance" (Deut. 21:22–23). Hellenization heightened the affront of crucifixion. Josephus tells how Alexander Jannaeus crucified 800 Jews:

> *His rage was grown so extravagant, that his*
> *barbarity proceeded to a degree of impiety;*
> *for when he had ordered eight hundred to be*
> *hung upon crosses in the midst of the city,*
> *he had the throats of their wives and chil-*
> *dren cut before their eyes; and these execu-*
> *tions he saw as he was drinking and lying*
> *down with his concubines. (Wars of the Jews*
> *1.4.6;* quoted from *The Life and Works of*
> *Flavius Josephus,* trans. William Whiston
> [Philadelphia: John C. Winston Company, n.d.])

Such an atrocity deepened Jewish feeling against Gentiles and their instrument of torture. Since the Jews thought of the Messiah in nationalistic terms, the idea that He should die on a cross was repulsive.

Jesus obviously knew that and made the cross one of the major themes of His ministry. The gospels make it abundantly clear that Jesus told His disciples that He was going to be put to death (Matt. 16:21 and par.; 17:12; 17:22–23 and par.; 20:17–19 and par.; 26:12; Mark 2:20; 9:12; 10:45; Luke 12:50; 22:15; etc.). In this week's Passion reading, Matthew 26:1–13, He indicates that His death will be by crucifixion. Mark tells us that Jesus' prediction at Caesarea Philippi was quite clear: "He spoke plainly about this" (Mark 8:32). Despite the plain and repeated predictions, the disciples appear totally confused by the events of Holy Week. Jesus didn't have the luxury of talking about different designs for crosses. The cross itself, in whatever shape, was hard for the disciples to deal with.

Context: Jesus and Nicodemus

One reason the disciples had difficulty was the Jewish religious establishment. John 3:1–13, the context preceding this week's sermon text, indicates that Nicodemus, "a member of the Jewish ruling council" (v. 1), was perplexed when Jesus taught him about regeneration and crucifixion. Jesus, in turn, was uneasy with Nicodemus's bewilderment: "You are Israel's teacher, and do you not understand these things?" (v. 10). "These things" are His teachings about the regenerative work of the Holy Spirit. "No one can enter the kingdom of God unless he is born of water and the Spirit" (v. 5).

The problem was not that Nicodemus and the rest of the establishment that he represents did not have sufficient information. The Old Testament could have prepared them for the teaching of Jesus. Rather, their problem was a rejection of Jesus. "I tell you the truth, we speak of what we know, and we testify to what we have seen, but still you people do not accept our testimony" (v. 11). Jesus' testimony is not just a human speculation; it is a revelation of the incarnate Son of Man: "No one has ever gone into heaven except the one who came from heaven—the Son of Man" (v. 13). What Jesus has to say about regeneration and the cross is confusing only to those who could not deny themselves for his sake.

Martin Luther used John 3:1–15 as his text for Trinity Sunday, 1526. He paraphrased Jesus' words, "I tell you the truth, no one can enter the kingdom of God unless he is born again," to contrast the self-centered Jewish system with His own fulfillment of the Law:

> *There, now, you hear what is my doctrine, about which you have inquired. I do not teach in opposition to the Law of God, to destroy it, but I only charge you with not having kept it, yea, with not understanding it, though you pretend to be its instructors and imagine that you are fulfilling it. You imagine that I ought to preach the Law the same as you do, and that if the laws of Moses, which you claim to have kept, are not sufficient, I ought to bring to you a new and better law teaching good works, just as you set up many self-elected works in addition to God's law, as though you had already fulfilled it. But I am not telling you of new articles, law or works, for those the Law enjoins are already more than you can do and keep. But I teach that you must become altogether different persons.*
> (John Nicholas Lenker, ed., *Sermons of Martin Luther,* trans. Lenker et al. [Grand Rapids, Mich.: Baker Book House, 1983], 3:426)

7

Jesus opposes the popular religion of glorious self-righteousness. He will not give Nicodemus or His disciples more of the same, no "new articles, law or works," but instead He draws out the true lesson of the Old Testament and of Numbers 21: "Just as Moses lifted up the snake in the desert, so the Son of Man must be lifted up, that everyone who believes in him may have eternal life" (vv. 14–15).

The Text: John 3:14–15

In Numbers 21 the Israelites, traveling around Edom, grumbled against God and Moses: "Why have you brought us up out of Egypt to die in the desert? There is no bread! There is no water! And we detest this miserable food!" (v. 5). The Lord responded by sending venomous snakes, whose bites caused many of the people to die (1 Cor. 10:9). When the people repented and sought Moses' intercession before the Lord, God told him: "Make a snake and put it up on a pole; anyone who is bitten can look at it and live" (v. 8).

Tradition says that Moses used the Tau Cross to fulfill these instructions. Tradition was also quick to find the deeper significance of the bronze snake: "For he who turned toward it was saved, not by what he saw, but by thee, the Savior of all" (Wisd. of Sol. 16:7). That passage is picked up in the Talmud: "Having a token of salvation, to put them in remembrance of Thy Law: for he that turned toward it was not saved because of that which was beheld, but because of thee, the Savior of all" (Rosh ha-Shanah 3.8).

The comparison between the wilderness incident and Jesus is in "lifted up" more so than in the object of crucifixion, Christ or the serpent. The word *hupsoō*, to lift up, is not uncommon in John. " 'But I, when I am lifted up from the earth, will draw all men to myself.' He said this to show the kind of death he was going to die" (John 12:32–33). "Jesus said, "When you have lifted up the Son of Man, then you will know that I am the one I claim to be and that I do nothing on my own but speak just what the Father has taught me" (8:28). That the comparison hinges on "lifted up" is apparent from Jesus' repetition of the verb: "Just as Moses lifted up the snake in the desert, so the Son of Man must be lifted up" (3:14). Early Christian writers like Barnabas (12.5–7), Justin (*Apol.* 60), and Tertullian (*Adv. Marc.* 3.18) interpreted the serpent as a type of Christ. But it is the action of being lifted up for sinners to behold and be saved that provides the type and antitype more than those who are lifted up.

Jesus gives the purpose of His comparison in v. 15: "That everyone who believes in him may have eternal life." The crucifixion is intended to call forth faith. Faith, in turn, brings eternal life, not because of the person who believes but because of the object, God and Christ, that is believed. Jesus does not delimit this in any way. *Pas ho pisteuōn* transcends Jew and Gentile, male and female, Pharisee, Sadducee, or any modern religious brand name. Faith and eternal life are for anyone. Take care to note the Johannine definition of "eternal life" as you prepare your sermon: "Now this is eternal life: that they may know you, the only true God, and Jesus Christ, whom you have sent" (17:3). This eternal life comes from the cross, the last place that people would have expected to find life. No wonder that Nicodemus and the disciples found the prophecies of the cross so difficult to comprehend!

But Christ's prophecies proved themselves to be true. People like Nicodemus and the disciples eventually believed. In John 3:2 Nicodemus came to Jesus by night, a Johannine literary device that indicates spiritual darkness (cf. 13:30). The next time that Nicodemus appears in the Gospel, he comes in daylight with Joseph of Arimathea and takes the body of Jesus from the cross. The evangelist seems to be suggesting that Nicodemus came to faith. We know that the disciples did also. Those prophecies of passion that were so difficult to comprehend at first became more obvious as time passed. Today we can look back and see how God fulfilled His word. May the crosses of Lent be a refreshing look back with promises of a glorious future!

Sermon Starters

Outline 1:   **Benefiting from Hindsight**

Central thought: Jesus' prophecies of the cross were difficult for many to understand. Their experiences help us in our faith.
  I. Introduction: Hindsight is 20/20
    A. Examples from daily life
    B. Applicable also to spiritual matters
    C. Lent is a time to learn from the experience of other Christians, like Nicodemus.
 II. Jesus prophesies His cross
    A. John 3:14
    B. Numbers 21:8–9
    C. Tau Cross: The cross of prophecy
III. Prophecies of the cross are not readily understood
    A. Nicodemus was bewildered.
    B. Disciples confused by passion predictions
    C. Two reasons:
      1. Repulsiveness of the cross
      2. Denies our merits before God
 IV. Jesus fulfilled His prophecies
    A. Lifted up on the cross, as he said
    B. Nicodemus and the other disciples eventually understood
  V. Benefiting from Hindsight
    A. Lent allows us to look back and learn
    B. Crosses of Lent will help us
    C. Goal: Eternal life, to know the Christ lifted up on the cross

Outline 2: "Turn to Me and Be Saved"

Central thought: Jesus' prophecies of the cross were intended for the salvation of sinners.
  I. Introduction: "Turn to me and be saved" (Is. 45:22)
    A. Our goal: For all to believe and have eternal life (John 3:15)
    B. Our program: The crosses of Lent
 II. Tau: The cross of prophecy
    A. Jesus prophesied His cross (John 3:14 et al.)
    B. Jesus fulfilled his prophecies
III. Purpose of the cross: "Turn to me and be saved"
    A. Numbers 21:8–9
    B. John 3:15
 IV. Lent: A time to call people to the crosses of Lent
    A. To call you
    B. To call a friend or relative

Outline 3: No "New Articles, Law or Works"

Central thought: What Jesus promised and did at the cross is unique.
  I. Introduction: Luther preached on Jesus' and Nicodemus' conversation.
    A. The cross is not just a new article, more Law and works
    B. Lent a time to worship at the cross, God's unique way of salvation
    C. The crosses of Lent
 II. Tau: The cross of prophecy
    A. Jesus prophesied His cross (John 3:14 et al).
    B. He promised to be lifted up for salvation (Num. 21:8–9)
III. People didn't expect cross prophecies
    A. Confusion of Nicodemus and the disciples
    B. Expected a "new article, law and works"
    C. What do you expect this Lent?
 IV. Prophecies fulfilled at the cross
    A. As in Numbers 21, Jesus was lifted up
    B. Place of agony
    C. Affront to the self-righteous
    D. Place of salvation (John 3:15)
  V. Conclusion: Lent, a time to worship at the unique cross

Sermon: The Cross of Prophecy

John 3:14–15; Num. 21:4–9

Predictions always fascinate us. We are very curious about what the future may have in store for us individually or for the world in general, so we always welcome an opportunity to get a peek into the future.

We get irritated when predicters prove to be wrong. We know that it is not possible for anybody to get an absolutely sure look into the future, but somehow it seems to us that if somebody proposes to give us a glimpse of the future, it is incumbent on that person to be pretty much on target. When the weather turns out other than what it is "supposed to" be, or if the economy turns in directions quite different from what financial advisers have suggested it would, we get upset. Sometimes we just laugh it off, but inside it disturbs us to be told one thing about the future and to have it turn out quite different.

Nothing is more predictable than death. One can predict that with the same certainty that one can predict the rising and setting of the sun. Even more confidently, in fact.

Interestingly enough, the very same death that we can so confidently predict is at the same time the hardest of all things in our human future to come to terms with. We know it lies there, but our neighbor's death is more sure than our own. We find it almost impossible to think of death as a real part of our own future, for we seem to feel in some peculiar way that we will be a notable exception to that universal rule.

The long-established practice of imposing ashes in a crude form of the cross on the forehead of church members on this day is designed to remind us that we are not immune to death. "Remember that you are dust, and to dust you shall return," the minister says to each one receiving the ashes. And with those ashes on your forehead, every glance in the mirror or every casual brush across the forehead reminds you by sight and touch of your mortality.

Prophecy and the Future

While we have been talking about predictions, note that we have not yet spoken of prophecies. Prophecy is something quite different from mere prediction even though the two words are often confused and sometimes even used as synonyms. A predicter is not necessarily a prophet, nor is a prophet necessarily a predicter. A prophet may make some predictions in connection with his larger message, but it is not necessary for the prophet to have predictions at the heart and core of the concerns he expresses.

The prophet is intent on interpreting a situation, on speaking a word that will help people understand what is going on within a given setting. If a prediction is involved, the prophetic word must explain why the prophet would make such a prediction. Any predictions that the prophet might make are not given to satisfy curiosity about the future. They are based on what is happening at a given moment, ways of saying, "Since this is true, contrary to the will of God (or sometimes, in accord with the will of God), then this and this is what you can expect." So the prophet was someone who interpreted the times and brought "the word of the Lord" into the situation.

Particular situations, in turn, are always part of larger situations. Therefore, "the word of the Lord" to a particular time or event must also be more significant than that one time or that single event. When the prophet addressed himself to the people in exile in Babylon, for example, he spoke of their previous waywardness as the cause of their exile. His word was shaped by that event as he interpreted their predicament. But then he took that moment and added hope as he addressed the Word of the Lord's promise to it. So the prophet took the present, interpreted it by remembering the past, and then directed the despairing people to their only source of hope: the very God who had claimed Israel as His own chosen nation.

Prophecy always had a hint of the future in it since it addressed the people, telling them what could happen by the grace of God. In general, therefore, it is a word from the Lord addressed to those who need to hear a word of grace, a word of redirection, a word of hope, a word of encouragement, a call to turn from former ways so that they could again serve the Lord in new ways. It was not a prediction made to satisfy curious minds, but it was a word of interpretation and hope designed to guide the people of God into His ways and away from the ways of human self-will.

The Text as Prophecy

All of this needs to be said so that we can better understand the words of Jesus that form our text for this evening. He refers to an event in the distant past as a prophetic event that helps His people understand who He is and what His task is all about.

The Original Event: Numbers 21

The historic event to which Jesus refers takes place during the 40 years of Israel's wandering in the desert. The long wait for the Promised Land was becoming tiresome. Life had lost its zest and the people had a hard time seeing the fulfillment of the Lord's promise. The present, therefore, had become a burden. "The people grew impatient on the way; they spoke against God and against Moses, and said, 'Why have you brought us up out of Egypt to die in the desert? There is no bread! There is no water! And we detest this miserable food!'" (Num. 21:4–5). Even the manna, once received gratefully, was now unwelcome.

So the Lord intervened. What appeared as punishment to some became a call to repentance to others. "Then the Lord sent venemous snakes among them; they bit the people and many Israelites died" (v. 6). When the Lord deals with a heavy hand, the results are consequential! He makes plain that He does not take the complaints of the Israelites lightly.

Nor does He come among them without result. "The people came to Moses and said, 'We sinned when we spoke against the Lord and against you' " (v. 7). They recognized the relationship between the snakes and their sin, so they did not simply set out on a program of snake eradication, nor did they suggest a move to a less dangerous place. They knew that when the Lord set out to call them back from their sin, He would pursue them no matter where they went or how many snakes they killed. The only thing to do was to confess their sin and pray for God's grace. So they did exactly that.

"The Lord said to Moses, 'Make a snake and put it up on a pole; anyone who is bitten can look at it and live.' So Moses made a bronze snake and put it up on a pole" (vv. 8–9). The Tau Cross that holds our attention this evening represents this event, for tradition says that this was the shape of the pole that Moses erected on which to place the bronze snake. It is also called the Old Testament Cross or the Egyptian Cross, presumably because it was the cross that saved the people on their way out of Egypt.

So the Lord provides a way of escape as Moses obediently follows His command, creating a human version of the snakes that threatened their lives. This one, though, was without poison and it was, as it were, a creation of the Lord himself through the hand of Moses to preserve His people.

"When anyone was bitten by a snake and looked at the bronze snake, he lived" (v.9), we are told. This was as wonderfully mysterious and unexplainable as the cross of Christ, for those who "look at the cross of Jesus," to use the language of the account in Numbers, will live even though they have been bitten by the snake of sin. The two accounts cross over and enrich one another!

As a serpent once whispered temptation, snakes now bit the people with deadly venom. A bronze snake is then raised on a Tau Cross to create that strange radiation of grace by which we all live! That is why the Tau Cross is considered by tradition to be the Prophecy Cross as Moses, lifting up the snake in the wilderness, portends the lifting up of Jesus on the cross outside the city gates of Jerusalem.

And the people are healed in a mysterious healing that comes to all who look at the snake out of desperation and penitence. It wasn't enough to admire the wonderful craftsmanship of Moses in the making of a bronze snake. When those bitten look in faith on this work of the Lord performed through His servant Moses, they are saved. The promise of God is attached to this snake. This promise draws people to it

Jesus' Encounter with Nicodemus: John 3

Here you gain insight into the text, which says, "As Moses lifted up the snake in the desert, so the Son of man must be lifted up, that everyone who believes in him may have eternal life" (John 3:14–15). These words lead to that familiar "Gospel in a nutshell" passage we use so often, pouring meaning into Jesus' statement that "God so loved the world that he gave his one and only Son, that whoever believes in him shall not perish but have eternal life." But remember: These words are spoken long before the cross is raised.

The conversation is spoken almost in whispers, under the cloak of night, around a small wick lighting the room where Nicodemus encounters Jesus. There, in the night silence, Nicodemus probes the question of who Jesus is and what He understands His mission to be. He has undoubtedly heard John the Baptizer's call to penitence and remembers that John pointed to one greater than he. Perhaps Nicodemus had witnessed Jesus' zeal when He cleansed the temple and sensed that this was not merely an overzealous radical taking up a religious cause. Quite the contrary. "We know you are a teacher who has come from God," Nicodemus whispers. "For no one could perform the miraculous signs you are doing if God were not with him" (v. 2). Jesus responds by talking about being "born again," an expression akin to John's call to repentance. Nicodemus cannot understand. Jesus presses the point. He speaks of the wonderfully unexplainable and mysterious way that God's Spirit moves into and through human history—like a wind moving mysteriously. "So it is with everyone born of the Spirit" (v. 8)

This is the context within which we hear of the snake in the wilderness and the raising of the Tau Cross, the Prophecy Cross. Jesus uses shorthand language in pointing to it, for Nicodemus knows the story well: "As Moses lifted up the snake in the desert, so the Son of Man must be lifted up, that everyone who believes in him may have eternal life" (vv. 14–15).

Could Nicodemus see already at that time, long before Jesus' crucifixion and resurrection, how intimately Jesus was connected to the bronze snake? Could he see by the flickering lamplight that, as the snake was a bronze image of the poisonous snakes, so also, sitting here before him was one even more like us humans than the bronze snake was like a snake? Could he catch a glimpse yet of what we confess about this ever-so-human brother, namely, that He alone was without the poison of the sin that destroys humankind, and therefore He alone could hang from a Tau Cross so that poisoned humans like you and me could look on Him and live?

Nicodemus floats hauntingly in and out of John's gospel, apparently growing in understanding and attaching himself closer and closer to Jesus even though remaining at a distance until, at the time of Christ's death, he openly and boldly confesses that attachment by providing the mixture of myrrh and aloes for His burial and helping to remove the body from that Tau Cross. As he carried that body, he surely must have remembered this conversation. Still the mystery surrounded it, of course, for until the resurrection, the death remained shrouded in darkness. But the conversation must have been ringing in his ears.

The Cross as Prophecy to Us

Surely by now you have found your place in this story, have you not? We have told it twice, but in relating it to your life, it must be told still a third time. It will interpret your life, interpret what God did for and among humankind in Christ, help you understand the way God intercepts your life, renews it, and acts within it. In short, it will now prophecy to you.

Surely the deadly snakes are a word of prophecy, are they not? Do you feel them slithering into your life as the sin that bites with deadly venom? Just when you think you are safest—while reading the evening newspaper or watching TV or doing your job or sitting quietly at the beach or strenuously exercising your body—the snake of sin slides quietly into your life and sinks its fangs into you. There is no need for you to frequent bars or gambling houses or special arenas of sin to feel the poisonous bite of these snakes of sin circulating in the wilderness of your daily life. Quietly, suddenly, but all-too-deadly, the bite comes, and the poison races through your blood even now.

But a voice is heard in the midst of the snakes, a voice calling you to penitence. It is the word that calls forth the raising up of the Tau Cross. It is the call from God, a word of prophecy. "Turn from your complaints and rebellion and self-will. Look on the bronze snake, the Man for all people, the second Adam. And when you look, the snakes will release you. The venom will be cleansed from your blood and you will live!" It is the word of hope. It is the Lord's doing, a deed of His making.

The pole on which the snake is raised blends in with the cross on which Jesus is raised. When you see this Man, fashioned by God in the womb of a woman and placed on a cross raised high for all to see, you see the grace of God raised high over the sins of humankind in one encapsuled moment. The blood of the Christ becomes the blood of the Passover Lamb placed on the doorposts of your heart.

This, too, is part of the tradition of the Tau Cross, the tradition that this was the image that was used when the blood of the Passover lamb was smeared on the doorposts of the Israelite houses. It is the mark by which the wrath and anger of God was turned away from them—and from you— and sent on its way. It is the sign of faith, the looking to the bronze snake and seeing there your hope and your life in the form of the Man of the Cross.

In Christ you have the ultimate word of what life is all about, for you see life lived as it should be when you watch Him. Through Him you see how God works to make this kind of life possible. This is what we learn on Ash Wednesday as the Word of Prophecy comes through the bronze snake, helping you thereby to understand the cross as your way from death in sin to life in God.

This life in Christ is a life of humility, of hope, of daily renewal and regeneration—even a life of suffering! All of these aspects of life will be considered through other forms of the cross to be explored in weeks to come. You will be surprised at how many forms of the cross there are, and you will discover many messages in them.

On this Ash Wednesday, though, we focus attention on the Tau Cross, the Cross of Prophecy. Here you find a powerful interpretation of the will of God—a will that sends grace into the midst of sin, a will that heals where mortal wounds have been inflicted, a will that mysteriously saves you in that wonderfully unexplainable way of God as you are led to look on the Man raised on the cross that you might not die but live.

This Cross of Prophecy is where life comes to be understood through death. Here God gives light for your way, hope for your life, strength for your journey. He raises it on a pole in the wilderness of life where snakes snap and bite. He urges you to look at it and live. "As Moses lifted up the snake in the desert, so the Son of man must be lifted up, that everyone who believes in him may have eternal life."

It is the Word of the Lord!

It is your word of life!

Week of Lent 1

Saltire Cross—Humility

Sermon Study

Text: Matthew 16:24–27
Passion Reading: John 13:1–20

Introduction

Humility can fool you. It's so easy to advocate it from the pulpit, so easy to hear about it from the pew, but so difficult to translate it into a consistent trait of character. Therein is the challenge for this week. The subject of humility is so natural for Lent. Note from the Passion reading that Jesus washes the disciples' feet—the kind of story we expect at this time of year. And pastoral exhortations to humility are often so stereotyped that our members could easily seem to be hearing and endorsing humility without beginning a serious examination of their lives.

The Saltire Cross is associated with humility because of Andrew. When facing martyrdom by crucifixion, he requested that his executioners not crucify him on the Latin cross, the form of the cross on which Christ had died. His request was allowed and the Saltire Cross was used. For this reason it is also known as St. Andrew's cross. Whatever the name, it symbolizes the humility that Andrew demonstrated throughout his life and that we will urge on our hearers.

If a sermon does nothing more than plant one small idea in the listener's mind, that sermon has done something great. Winston Churchill did that for many people when he said, "(Clement) Atlee is a very modest man— and with reason." May the Holy Spirit help your sermon to plant humility, a humility caused less by our shortcomings and more by our admiration for Jesus, who "humbled himself and became obedient to death—even death on a cross!" (Phil. 2:8).

Background: Humble, Helpful Andrew

Though overshadowed by his brother Peter's dominant personality, Andrew's humility was very effective in the early days of the church. Andrew and Peter were sons of a man named John (John 1:42) and came from Bethsaida, a city east of Capernaum on the Sea of Galilee. In the gospels we find the brothers living in Capernaum, no doubt because they and their fishing partners, Zebedee, James, and John (Mark 1:16–20; Luke 5:10), found it advantageous to be on the heavily traveled *Via Maris*.

Andrew was a follower of John the Baptist and perhaps one of his closest disciples (John 1:35). That association tells us that Andrew gladly received the preaching of repentance, either because he was naturally humble, self-effacing, and aware of his sin, or because he was humbled by the strong preaching of John. In either case, a repentant Andrew heard John call Jesus "the Lamb of God" (v. 36). Andrew followed Jesus to his place of lodging in Judea and spent the day with him. The evangelist reports: "It was about the tenth hour" (v. 39), perhaps a symbolical statement of fulfillment (Bultmann). Their time together convinced Andrew that Jesus is the Christ, and so he went and told his brother, Peter, "We have found the Messiah," and literally led Peter to Jesus (John 1:40—42). Peter was not the only one whom Andrew introduced to Jesus. In John 12:22 he introduced some Greeks to the Savior. Andrew also introduced Jesus to the lad with five loaves and two small fish when the 5,000 needed food. For these reasons the Venerable Bede called Andrew "the Introducer." It is the kind of helpful action we would expect from one who is humble.

Where Biblical facts leave off, tradition picks up. Andrew is reputed to have become an apostle to the Scythians, which helps explain why he is the patron saint of Hungary and Russia. Other traditions locate his activity in the northern provinces of Asia Minor, perhaps in association with his brother Peter (cf. 1 Peter 1:1). Jerome says that he preached in Achaia in Greece, a tradition preserved by Abdias, who relates the interesting account of Andrew's death on the Saltire Cross.

It seems that the preaching and miracles performed by Andrew made converts of many of the inhabitants of the town of Patras. The proconsul Aegeas, in an attempt to restore the ancestral pagan cults, summoned Andrew before him for an attack on the Christian Gospel. Andrew was jailed, the Christian citizenry enraged, and a riot would have broken out had not Andrew urged the people to imitate the patience and humility of the Savior. Tensions continued to escalate until Aegeas decreed Andrew's death. Consistent with his humility, he asked that he not die on the same shape cross on which Jesus had died. The request was granted, the Saltire Cross prepared, and tradition says that Andrew greeted the cross with these words:

> *Hail, precious cross, that hast been conse-*
> *crated by the body of my Lord, and adorned*
> *with His limbs as with rich jewels. I come to*
> *thee exulting and glad; receive me with joy*
> *into thy arms. O, good cross, that hast re-*
> *ceived beauty from our Lord's limbs: I have*
> *ardently loved thee. Long have I desired and*
> *sought thee; now thou art found by me, and*
> *art made ready for my longing soul: receive*
> *me into thine arms, take me from among*
> *men, and present me to my Master; that He*
> *who redeemed me on thee, may receive me*
> *by thee.*

He died on November 30, a day preserved in the church calendar as the Day of St. Andrew.

Context: More Than Lip Service to Humility

There's no reason to doubt that Andrew was present at Caesarea Philippi when Jesus questioned the disciples about his identity. If Andrew had been closely associated with John the Baptist, he certainly was with Jesus. In the Synoptics he is always listed among the first four disciples, and in Matthew and Luke he is one of the first two. Though Peter is the only disciple whose speech is personally recorded, Andrew may well have answered Jesus' question, "Who do people say the Son of Man is?" (Matt. 16:13). When Jesus had taken that poll of public opinion, He zeroed in on the disciples: "Who do you say I am?" (v. 15). Brother Peter answered, not just for himself but as spokesman for the Twelve: "You are the Christ, the Son of the living God" (v. 16).

That answer was correct, but there was still plenty of confusion about the function of the Messiah. That Peter did not understand the work of the Messiah is evident from verse 22, where he reacts to Jesus' Passion prediction and misses the promise of the resurrection. Since the disciples did not understand that the Messiah must suffer, they misconceived their own roles as followers of Jesus. Thus at Caesarea Philippi Jesus drew an important corollary about humility from His own experience at the cross: "If anyone would come after me, he must deny himself and take up his cross and follow me" (v. 24). Lessons on humility were as much standard fare in first century Judaism as in 20th century Christianity, but Jesus' teaching at Caesarea Philippi led to the disciples' eventual realization that more than lip service to humility is required if you are going to walk the way of the cross.

Old Testament teachings about humility were rooted in the real life origins of Israel: "The Egyptians mistreated us and made us suffer, putting us to hard labor" (Deut. 26:6). Lest their release from oppression encourage pride, God used the wilderness wanderings to humble Israel: "Remember how the Lord your God led you all the way in the desert these forty years, to humble you and to test you in order to know what was in your heart" (8:2; cf. also v. 16). Humility, expressed either by its original denotation of poverty or figuratively by a meek character, is a mark of the saved: "You save the humble, but your eyes are on the haughty to bring them low" (2 Sam. 22:28). The prophets continued the contrast between the poor and the powerful, and Jesus picked up the theme in His ministry (Is. 3:14–15; Jer. 2:34; Amos 2:6–7).

St. Matthew's gospel presents humility as one of the issues of conflict between Jesus and the Pharisees. Just before Jesus stings the Pharisees with seven woes in chapter 23, He described them as self-aggrandizing teachers of religion, whose example should not be followed by His disciples.

> *You are not to be called "Rabbi," for you*
> *have only one Master and you are all broth-*
> *ers. And do not call anyone on earth*
> *"father," for you have one Father, and he is*
> *in heaven. Nor are you to be called*

> *"teacher," for you have one Teacher, the*
> *Christ. The greatest among you will be your*
> *servant. For whoever exalts himself will be*
> *humbled, and whoever humbles himself will*
> *be exalted. (Matt. 23:8–12)*

To be sure, the rabbis were not in the habit of preaching haughtiness. The Talmud, the 63-book of commentary and discussion on the Torah, contains many exhortations to humility. "Why are the words of the Law likened unto water (Is. 55:1)? Because, like water, it will not abide in high places, but in low ones" (*Taanith*, fol. 7, col. 1). Another rabbinic teaching on humility:

> *For four reasons does the substance of*
> *wealthy people go to ruin: Because they de-*
> *lay paying the wages of their hired laborers;*
> *because they withhold them altogether; be-*
> *cause they remove the yokes from their own*
> *necks and put them upon those of their fel-*
> *lows; and on account of pride, which is as*
> *bad as all the rest put together; but concern-*
> *ing the meek it is written (Ps. 37:11): "The*
> *meek shall inherit the earth." (Sucah, fol. 29,*
> col. 2)

Though these quotations postdate Jesus' ministry on earth, the conservative nature of rabbinic pedagogy assures us that His contemporaries advocated such humility in their teaching. Jesus himself said, "You must obey them and do everything they tell you. But do not do what they do, for they do not practice what they preach" (Matt. 23:3).

The problem then is the same problem that faces you as you prepare to preach on humility. Intellectual assent to the concept of humility is quite expected in Judeo-Christian circles. For Christians it is almost a commonplace topic for Lent, the time when we routinely exhort the congregation to imitate the selflessness of Christ. But a public faith without works is dead, and a member whose character or life-style is not humble needs to struggle with the call of humility just as Andrew, Peter, and the other disciples did. This is your challenge as you prepare for the pulpit.

Text: Matthew 16:24–27

> *Then Jesus said to his disciples, "If anyone*
> *would come after me, he must deny himself*
> *and take up his cross and follow me. For*
> *whoever wants to save his life will lose it,*
> *but whoever loses his life for me will find it.*
> *What good will it be for a man if he gains*
> *the whole world, yet forfeits his soul? Or*
> *what can a man give in exchange for his*
> *soul? For the Son of Man is going to come in*
> *his Father's glory with his angels, and then*

he will reward each person according to
what he has done."

Verse 24: "Then Jesus said to his disciples, 'If anyone would come after me, he must deny himself and take up his cross and follow me.' " The word for humility, *tapeinos,* is not used, but the concept is manifestly present. Cf. 10:38–39. Jesus has predicted His own cross (16:21) and now urges the disciples to assume the crosses unique to their own lives. Such self-denial can result only in total dependence on God (cf. Deut. 7:7–8; Micah 6:8). St. Luke's account adds the word "daily": "take up his cross daily and follow me" (Luke 9:23). That adverb is a favorite of St. Luke and makes the good point that humility is a constant mark of discipleship, not just a periodic religious utterance. On the whole verse, see Galatians 2:20: "I have been crucified with Christ and I no longer live, but Christ lives in me. The life I live in the body, I live by faith in the Son of God, who loved me and gave himself for me."

Verse 25 presents a paradox: "For whoever wants to save his life will lose it, but whoever loses his life for me will find it." The critical words here are "for me," *heneken emou.* Compare the saying of Rabbi Yose in the early second century after Christ: "Whoever exalts himself above the words of the Law shall be abased at last, and he that abases himself for the sake of the words of the Law, shall be exalted in the end" (*Avoth* of Rabbi Nathan, ch. 11). Jesus' conflict with the Pharisees is not simply their failure to practice what they preach but ultimately their soteriology.

Verse 26: "What good will it be for a man if he gains the whole world, yet forfeits his soul? Or what can a man give in exchange for his soul?" Life with God is infinitely more valuable than the material or social offerings of this world. That is why both testaments are so kindly disposed toward the poor and humble. Externals like money, prestige, and power are not the essence of the soul and cannot redeem life. "The ransom for a life is costly, no payment is ever enough" (Ps. 49:8). The rich man and poor Lazarus could be a useful illustration (Luke 16:19–31).

Verse 27 reminds us that we live in view of judgment: "For the Son of Man is going to come in his Father's glory with his angels, and then he will reward each person according to what he has done." Judaism made a distinction between an earthly Messiah who would suffer and the heavenly Messiah who would not. But Jesus is one and the same.

"The high priest asked him, 'Are you the Christ, the Son of the Blessed One?' "

" 'I am,' said Jesus. 'And you will see the Son of Man sitting at the right hand of the Mighty One and coming on the clouds of heaven" (Mark 14:61–62).

The glorious, heavenly Messiah is also humble!

With "according to what he has done" Jesus quotes Psalm 62:12: "Surely you will reward each person according to what he has done." This is not work-righteousness, for deeds issue from repentant faith (Matt. 3:8), "and without faith it is impossible to please God" (Heb. 11:6).

This was not the first time that Jesus had attacked the Pharisees' lack of humility. While they laid heavy burdens on the people, Jesus had told his followers that "my yoke is easy and my burden is light" (Matt. 11:30). He presented himself as the paradigm of humility: "Take my yoke upon you and learn from me, for I am gentle and humble in heart, and you will find rest for your souls" (v. 29). On another occasion, the disciples asked a question appropriate for theologians of glory: "Who is the greatest in the kingdom of heaven?" (18:1). Jesus summoned a little child and said, "Whoever humbles himself like this child is the greatest in the kingdom of heaven" (v. 4). Identifying himself with the humble, he immediately added, "and whoever welcomes a little child like this in my name welcomes me" (v. 5). This week's Passion reading, the washing of the disciples' feet, is a graphic presentation of Jesus' consistent teaching on His humility and the humility of His disciples.

> *"Do you understand what I have done for you?" he asked them. "You call me 'Teacher' and 'Lord,' and rightly so, for that is what I am. Now that I, your Lord and Teacher, have washed your feet, you also should wash one another's feet. I have set you an example that you should do as I have done for you."*
> *(John 13:12–15)*

Sermon Starters

Central thought: Jesus calls His followers to humility, to cross-bearing.

Outline 1: **From Gold-Bearer to Cross-Bearer**
I. Introduction
    A. A deceitful slave in Plautus' *Bacchides* says "My master will immediately change me from a gold-bearer to a cross-bearer."
    B. That's the change our Master wants: Humble Christians who bear the cross.
    C. The Saltire Cross symbolizes humility.
II. The Lesson of Caesarea Philippi
    A. Jesus is the Messiah.
    B. His disciples follow Him humbly to the cross.
    C. He offers a lesson and an example.
        1. Foot-washing
        2. Philippians 2:5–11 et al.
III. The Humility of Andrew
    A. He was present when Jesus taught and practiced humility.
    B. There are several Biblical examples of Andrew's humility.
    C. Tradition depicts his humility in the Saltire Cross.
IV. Conclusion
    A. Plautus's slave feared becoming a cross-bearer.
    B. Andrew's example encourages us to humbly and gladly bear our crosses.

Outline 2:   **"Hail, Precious Cross!"**

I. Introduction
   A. Andrew's greeting of the Saltire Cross
   B. How could anyone greet the instrument of death? With humility!
II. Andrew was humble.
   A. Bible examples of Andrew's humility
   B. Traditional events preceding his greeting and death on the Saltire Cross
III. Andrew learned humility from Jesus.
   A. Jesus' teaching at Caesarea Philippi
      1. Jesus is the Messiah.
      2. His followers humbly bear the cross.
   B. Jesus' example
      1. Foot-washing
      2. Philippians 2:5–11 et al.
IV. Hail, Precious Cross!
   A. Greet the crosses of your life.
   B. Greet them humbly.
   C. Greet them remembering Andrew and the Saltire Cross.

Outline 3:   **Let an X Mark the Spot**

I. Introduction
   A. X marks the spot on treasure maps.
   B. The Saltire Cross, an X, symbolizes humility, a real treasure in Christian life.
II. Jesus taught and demonstrated humility for you.
   A. Teaching humility: Caesarea Philippi
   B. Demonstrating humility: Foot-washing
   C. Philippians 2:5–11
   D. For you, salvation
III. Andrew is an example of X marking the spot.
   A. The Biblical record gives an example of his humility.
   B. Traditions about Andrew demonstrate his humility, especially his death on the Saltire Cross.
IV. Let an X mark your life!
   A. Churchill on Atlee
   B. Why you and I are humble
   C. Let X mark the spot!

Sermon: The Cross of Humility

Matthew 16:24–27

Were I to tell you that light is darkness, that black is white, or that up is down, I could not turn the world more upside down for you than the cross does! The cross so reverses all earthly systems that one can hardly comprehend how totally opposite it is from those systems with which we are accustomed to living. When Christ stresses the way of self-imposed weakness, of self-forfeiture, of losing one's life to gain it, of self-denial, of humility, He overturns everything the world tries to impress on us. It is like saying that light is darkness or that up is down.

The problem is simply that when everything is overturned by the cross, those things that appear to be weaknesses to the world come out as "virtues." That is what makes them seem so ridiculous. How can there be strength in humility, which is regarded as weakness? The world wants us to be modest, of course, which means we should *appear* to be humble. But when one actually *acts* humbly, the world interprets it as a lack of courage and strength—a way of cowardice and weakness, in fact. Who wants to lie down before life and let it walk all over you? Or who respects anyone who does that?

But Jesus insists that the way of humility is precisely the way of strength and courage. He shows how humility that leads to service is, in fact, a way of living with power. This is the very truth to which our text this evening points us. It tells us that humility is that courageous act of strength by which we give away all claims on life in order that our life might be grounded in God alone.

This truth is not easily absorbed, of course. Everyday experience offers quite a different view of humility and life than this. Because this is true, we must concentrate intense attention initially on the One who gave this instruction so that we can find from His life what all this means.

The Imprint of Humility on the Life of Christ

One simple fact will quickly catch the attention of anyone who reads the accounts of Christ's life in the gospels: Jesus never sought anything for Himself by the way He lived and worked among people. The narratives all tell of a self-giving man whose entire attention was devoted to giving Himself away. What He did was designed to help others, not to gain something for Himself personally.

There are occasions when people wanted to reward Him. Even the Tempter himself was willing to "reward" Jesus from the beginning of His ministry if only Jesus would do his bidding in the simplest way. "Why a cross when You can have all the world from my hand just for the asking?" the Tempter asks. It would only take a small symbolic gesture for Jesus to bypass the cross and everything that went with it. The crowds speak the same way after He has fed them with some loaves of bread and a few small fish. They want to make Him a king. The question surely must have haunted Him in Gethsemane when the fullness of His suffering was beginning to bear down on Him. Only a few days earlier, on Palm Sunday, it was plain that He could have whatever He wanted from the people. They would have accepted Him as a "savior from Rome" on the spot that day. He had frustrated them by not accepting such an offer and walking away from it. But here in Gethsemane when the burden bears heavily, must He not have remembered the willing offers of the crowds? Why this when He could have had that? Even on the cross He endured the taunting jeers of those who offered to believe in Him if only He would come down off the cross, assert Himself, show some kind of kingly sign. Given the choice of a cross or a crown, what would *you* have done? Because we know what Jesus did, it seems hard to recognize that He had alternatives, options to exercise other than the one He chose—and tempting options, at that.

But Jesus was committed to only one thing—service to His heavenly Father. He devoted Himself to prayer, searched out the ways in which the Father led Him, "emptied" Himself of His own will so that there was room for the will of the Father to be exercised. A curt "It is written" was His response to every temptation, but it also shows the direction He set for His life.

This dogged determination to pursue the will of the Father marked His way from the cradle to the cross. Terrible though His cry of God-forsakenness was when He was enthroned on the cross, those who knew the Scriptures recognized His words as the opening words of Psalm 22, a psalm of torment and at the same time a psalm of hope and confidence. The word of the Lord sustained Him in the very moment when the powers of darkness were doing their utmost to devastate and destroy Him.

Doing "the things of God" involved far more than little exercises in piety. It meant more to Jesus than just reading the Scriptures daily or faithful attendance at synagogue. These things had their place and were important in Jesus' commitment to knowing and doing the will of the Father, but they enabled Him to turn outward again in concern for those around Him. Serving God meant loving care for those who needed Him.

The vital point of all this is that Jesus gave Himself freely in all of life (not just in death). Nothing—not even His life—was taken from Him by force. He did everything from strength, from a will committed to others even though it could have been turned in on Himself or at least withheld from those to whom He so freely gave. He was His "own person," to use the common language of today. But He was His "own person" in quite a different way from the way in which we commonly use the term. Being His "own person" meant that He gave His life as He pleased to God and for others out of a deep inner strength. He set Himself to live a life of total giving.

This is how the life and death of Jesus turned the world upside down as much as if He had said that light was darkness. The world understands being one's "own person" to mean making up one's own mind without the influence of others. It means setting one's own course in whatever direction one chooses without outside interference. Jesus does just the opposite when He claims to be his own person, for He places His personhood at the disposal of the Father. He would not set His own standards, nor would He let anybody else—not even mighty Rome—set them for Him. Not even death could set His standards; rather, He set the standards for death. Only the Father set Jesus' standards.

That is why we find Him so often in prayer, so intent on responding to temptation with His curt, "It is written," so devoted in His entire being to living out the humanity that was first given to Adam and Eve. That is why Paul refers to Him as the second Adam (1 Cor. 15:45). He was a Son of God as all children of God were meant to be when He placed the fullness of His humanity at the disposal of the Father. That is what it means to be human in the most complete sense of the term—not to do what we want to do but to do what the Father wills for us to do. We know our humanity best when we are closest to God and carrying out His will.

In the act of giving Himself to all people, Jesus became the person for all people, the One in whom all humanity could find its true purpose and through whom full humanity could be restored among us. When Jesus placed Himself squarely in the place of all others, you can see what His free, self-willing gift of Himself was all about. St. Paul, writing of Jesus to the Philippians, says, "Being in very nature God, [he] did not consider equality with God something to be grasped, but made himself nothing, taking the very nature of a servant" (Phil. 2:6–7). He was not torn loose from the glory of His Godhead after a mighty struggle; He gladly and willingly gave up that post to become the Man for all people. He came from strength with strength.

That is what made His humility so remarkable. It was not a result of weakness nor was it a weakness beyond His power to change. It is a self-imposed weakness, thereby overturning all the world's ideas about strength and its consequences. He proposed that saving the world must be done from a position of servanthood, from a stance of giving—even if it means giving up one's life.

If ever the values of the world have been turned topsy-turvy, it happened in this Man of Nazareth, whose throne was a cross and whose crown was made of thorns.

And we are to be like Him. We are to follow in His footsteps.

The Imprint of Jesus' Humility on One Who Followed Him

The form of the cross to which our attention is drawn in this service is formally called the Saltire Cross, although a more common name is the Cross of St. Andrew. Little is known of the later life of Andrew, brother of Peter, but a very old tradition says that Andrew was martyred by crucifixion. On that occasion, it is said, he pleaded himself unworthy to die in the same way that Jesus died, so they crucified him on an X-shaped cross such as you see in the Saltire Cross. The same tradition speaks of Andrew as a man of deep humility, and hence the cross is also often called the Cross of Humility, since it marks in some particular ways the life and death of one of our Lord's apostles. Still other traditions have connected those who were instructed by Andrew with the Christianizing of Scotland. The flag of Scotland has this cross imbedded in that country's national standard. So this form of the cross has spoken across the centuries and around the world in forceful ways of Christian humility.

This cross calls you to follow in the footsteps of the disciple after whom it is named. He had learned the secret of humility from Jesus Himself. He had taken seriously the words, "Take up your cross and follow me." The Saltire Cross calls on you to do the very same thing.

Humility: A Way of Life

One of the first things you learn from Jesus on the Cross of Humility is the simple yet profound truth that in reality you have no life to give away. Your life did not self-originate nor is it sustained apart from the Giver of life. The life you are to "deny" and "lose" is itself from God and is only on loan, as it were, to you. Your life belongs to God from its beginning; it is not yours to do with as you please.

That essential truth lies at the heart of the power we see in Christ. A basic reason He could never be cowed by those who threatened Him was that He never claimed to own His life in the first place. You threaten a person by telling him/her that you will take away some comfort, some money, some possession or life itself if he/she does not do your bidding. But how do you threaten a person who claims to own nothing? You cannot take anything away from a person who owns nothing. If even His life really belonged to the Father, who could do with it as He willed, Jesus was strangely beyond threat from those of this world.

You learn from Jesus that life as you experience it is "on loan" from the Father and is not really yours anyway. The only power you have is to determine who will, in the end, have any say over your life. You can wrench it away from God and give it to someone or something else that offers it security. Or you can leave it in the hands of its Maker and trust Him to care for it. To "have faith" is purely and simply to believe and live as though God alone has claim on your life and to reserve it in all its parts for His use.

Having established that fundamental understanding, it seems a contradiction to say that your life does, indeed, belong to you because God hands it over to you so that you might responsibly use it to His honor. He who owns it gives it into your care with the understanding that you must one day give an account of what you have done with it. Jesus speaks of this responsibility in our text: "The Son of man is going to come in his Father's glory with his angels, and then he will reward each person according to what he has done" (Matt. 16:27). So you are asked to make a major decision: What will you do with the life that God has planted into your body as His gift to you?

To deal with that question you must make an honest inventory of what God has given to you. This is not the time for false humility, denying what you have, or wishing for someone else's gifts while neglecting your own. This is the time for a full appraisal of God's gifts, a time for candor, for being honest with yourself about where your capabilities lie. Humility requires affirming what God has given to you so that it is openly at your disposal.

It is only when you know in true humility the strengths God has given to you that you can know what lies at your disposal for giving to others.

27

Consider: If Christ had denied what was given to Him, He could never have served us. He would have ended up a forgotten carpenter in Nazareth and the world would still be in darkness. Only the most intense honesty about the gifts God has given you can make you available for other people. You can lead from strength only when you know your strength.

Once that all comes clear, the final step in humility must take place. This is the step of determining how these gifts can be turned to the good of others. They are not given for self-service but for service to husband, wife, children, neighbors, community, the needy, the voiceless, the powerless, the wounded, the miserable. When you see your gifts through the lenses of such brothers and sisters, you begin to see into the gifts at your disposal with the same kind of vision that led Andrew to the Humility Cross and that led Jesus to the cross of your salvation.

On Saving Your Life By Losing It

Here you catch a glimpse into the deepest part of the text's urgent admonition to deny yourselves. Jesus is not simply promoting little programs of self-denial by which you give the money you would have spent on candy to the hungry or the time you would have spent at a movie in volunteer service at the Boys' Club. Rather, it is a whole way of life, or to use Jesus' words, it is a way of losing one's life to Him who is life itself. There is a sense in which it is an act of strength, for it means that you give your life over to God, who is far larger than your own little petty projects. On the other hand it is an act of the mercy of God, who calls you from petty projects into the service of all those around you in the name of Jesus Christ.

The closer you get to this One, who gave His life away with such strength, the more you will know the truth of what He says when He tells you that it profits us none to gain the whole world while forfeiting our life.

At the same time you will find His strength in you as you grow closer to Him. For when Christ lives in you, He who gave Himself away to others with such immense strength begins to stir things up in you so that your life, affected and changed by Him, turns outward to those who need the strength of your life. Life filled with Christ's life no longer has room for the old person; a new being lays claim to all that you do. He who comes to you in the words of Scripture and who comes to you through the tangible, earthly forms of the sacraments will draw you up into a vision of and participation in a life beyond anything you can imagine.

It looks so risky at first when you are told to give away all that has made your life secure. The world reminds you of that. It keeps calling to you, telling you that nothing can give you the security you have known through its treasures.

That is why you cannot simply look at the way, but you must rather look at the One who calls you. If you want courage to travel this way, watch Jesus mounting the Cross of Humility, entrusting Himself to the Father in death. Watch what happens to Him when He walks this upside-down way. If it proves safe for Him, will it not be safe for you, also?

"Whoever wants to save his life will lose it, but whoever loses his life for me will find it." It is the journey of Lent, this journey of the cross. And if you will travel it with Jesus, take your first step by His side this very evening!

Week of Lent 2

Anchor Cross—Hope

Sermon Study

Text: Hebrews 6:13–20
Passion Reading: Mark 14:43–52

Introduction

"In the sure and certain hope of the resurrection to eternal life," read the words of committal in the *Lutheran Agenda.* On a recent vacation to New England, I found a fisherman's grave marked by a stone inscribed with a lobster boat. A midwestern cemetery has a farmer's grave with a stone depicting a prize-winning steer. What kind of hope filled the lives of these men? By contrast, there is the grave of Dolly Pickett in Newburyport, Massachusetts. Her gravestone depicts a young woman standing and looking at sand passing through an hourglass. There is more, however, than the standard theme of *tempus fugit.* Though standing, the young woman is leaning against a large anchor. Over the entire scene are words from this week's Lenten text: "We have this hope as an anchor for the soul" (Heb. 6:19).

Christian hope is an anchor to lean on in this troubled life. That's why the people of Christ lay their loved ones to rest in that "sure and certain hope." This hope is dependable not because of our own efforts but because it is "built on nothing less than Jesus' blood and righteousness." The sureness of our hope is symbolized by the Anchor Cross. This cross goes back to the days of persecution before Constantine. To non-Christians the symbol appeared to be only an anchor, but to Christians it was a symbol of hope. The task this week is to invite your people to seize this hope. If they do not, their confidence will be lacking or misfounded as they face life's trials. The hopes of many people today are no more dependable than the lobster boat or steer marking their sad graves. May your proclamation of the Word result in a congregation with "throats that shout the hope that fills us."

Background: Hope and the Certainty of Salvation

Hope is a fickle quantity today. "I hope the weather will warm up soon." "I hope the Red Sox will win." If these hopes are fulfilled, fine. If not, life goes on. The impotence of this concept of hope shows when Christians are asked about the certainty of their salvation. "Are you going to heaven?" "I hope so" is often the tentative answer. That's not much of a hope, not much of an anchor to lean on.

The rabbis also were not sure of their salvation. Rabbi Jochanan ben Zakkai lived at the time of the apostles. On his deathbed he said, "There are two ways before me, the one to the Garden of Eden, the other to

Gehinnom, and I do not know on which they lead me. How can I help weeping?" In the third century another rabbi, also named Jochanan, asked to be buried neither in white clothes nor black because he did not know whether he would spend eternity with the righteous or sinners.

The uncertainty of these rabbis about salvation can be traced to their reliance on works. The pious deeds they performed as the children of Abraham were the basis of their salvation. In that sense they even claimed Habbakuk 2:4 as a dear passage. "The righteous will live by his faith" meant that righteousness is secured by faithful obedience to the Law. But a salvation that rests on pious works must always leave doubt. Have I done enough? Luther's monastic experience is confirming proof. Because of their reliance on works, the rabbis had no concept of hope. The Biblical concept and even the words of hope are lacking in their literature. Works are not a sure and steadfast anchor.

The Bible does speak of hope, but it's not the weak concept of so many people today. It is the basis of Christian life (Prov. 23:18). Without it, life is not worth living (Lam. 3:18). Biblical hope is such a strong factor in Christian living because it is directed toward God, not toward us. "Why are you downcast, O my soul? Why so disturbed within me? Put your hope in God, for I will yet praise him, my Savior and my God" (Ps. 42:11; cf. 1 Peter 1:21). This hope makes for vibrant, buoyant living because of the resurrection of Jesus Christ from the dead. "Praise be to the God and Father of our Lord Jesus Christ! In his great mercy he has given us new birth into a living hope through the resurrection of Jesus Christ from the dead" (1 Peter 1:3; cf. Luke 24:13–32). Luther: "One can judge what true Christian doctrine or preaching is. For when one wants to preach the Gospel, one must treat only of the resurrection of Christ.... For this is the chief article of our faith.... If there were no resurrection, we would have no consolation or hope" (The Catholic Epistles, trans. Martin H. Bertram; ed. Jaroslav Pelikan, Walter A. Hansen. Luther's Works, American Edition [St. Louis: Concordia Publishing House, 1967], 30:12).

Context: The Purpose of Hebrews

Hope dependable as an anchor was what the audience of the writer to the Hebrews needed. Bypassing the classical isagogical questions (Who wrote the book? Where did the people to whom it was addressed live? Is the superscription accurate?), it is generally agreed that the purpose of the letter was to encourage the faith of the recipients. "Brothers, I urge you to bear with my word of exhortation" (Heb. 13:22). These recipients were Jewish Christians who were being tempted to turn away from Christianity and revert to Judaism. In the past they had indeed demonstrated faith and love: "God is not unjust; he will not forget your work and the love you have shown him as you have helped his people and continue to help them" (6:10). Their efforts seem to be flagging, however. "Strengthen your feeble arms and weak knees" (12:12). "In your struggle against sin, you have not yet resisted to the point of shedding your blood" (v. 4). That the focus of temptation is a reversion of Judaism is suggested by the argument of the book. The superiority of Christ and Christianity is the major theme. The book does not begin with the traditional epistolary introduction (sender, addressees, saluation) but launches into a discussion of Christ's superiority over previous revelations (1:1–3), angels (1:4–2:18), Moses (3:1–19), and Joshua (4:1–13). These passages are all interspersed with exhortations (2:1–4, 3:1, 3:7–4:13).

The more immediate context for this week's sermon text is 4:14–7:28. The superior priesthood of Christ is the topic of 4:14–5:10. At that point the author begins an excursus against apostasy. He encourages his readers to be mature, to move beyond elementary teachings about Christ (6:1). Then he moves to a discussion of hope, their anchor that is firm and secure.

The situation of these Jewish Christians must be appreciated. To the people of the Roman Empire, Christianity is still a new religion. The lack of any reference in the book to the destruction of the temple suggests that it was written before A.D. 70. Christianity is new and growing, but Judaism has a longer, richer history and enjoys Roman protection. This would certainly entice some Christians to think about a return to their old ways of belief and worship. Perhaps some even did (6:4–8). The situation is not unlike people in our day and age who change churches and eventually have second thoughts. Their older church was more familiar, more comfortable. Perhaps Lutheran doctrine, which seemed so faithful to Scripture, wasn't reason enough to change. Perhaps we should accommodate faith and sight. Our people still need an anchor, a hope in the promises of God.

Text: Hebrews 6:11–20

Verse 12: "We do not want you to become lazy, but to imitate those who through faith and patience inherit what has been promised." The mention of faith, patience, inheritance, and promise in this exhortation sets the stage for our text.

In verses 13–15 Abraham is introduced as an example of faith and patience in awaiting the inheritance promised to him by God: "When God made his promise to Abraham, since there was no one greater for him to swear by, he swore by himself, saying, 'I will surely bless you and give you many descendants.' And so after waiting patiently, Abraham received what was promised." God's covenantal promise to Abraham (Gen. 22:16) was as relevant for the readers of Hebrews as it is for us today. The fulfillment of God's promises often seems so distant that it becomes very easy to accommodate ourselves to some present evil. For Abraham, as for the Hebrews and for us, the promise has its fulfillment in the future and may present nothing concrete for the present except the speaker's intention to fulfill his commitment. Thus living on a promise literally means living by faith and not by sight. In order that Abraham should not regard God's promise of many descendants as an empty promise, God swears to the promise by Himself.

The ancients took their oaths far more seriously than moderns. That is not necessarily an indictment of the ancients. Even when they made an oath in error, they regarded it as binding (Gen. 27:1–37; Num. 23; Judg. 11:29–40). In the Old Testament God Himself takes oaths. In Psalm 95:11 an oath climaxes God's review of His displeasure with Israel in the wilderness: "So I declared on oath in my anger, 'They shall never enter my rest' " (cf. Joshua 21:43; Num. 14:23, 29–30; Deut. 8:1). In our text the oath underscores the dependability of God's promise, a promise that is already sure because it comes from God Himself. God wants us to know that His promise is dependable, "an anchor for the soul, firm and secure" (Heb. 6:19).

In verses 16–18 the author expands on the previous thoughts by saying that God swore the highest possible oath when He swore by Himself: "Men swear by someone greater than themselves, and the oath confirms what is said and puts an end to all argument. Because God wanted to make the unchanging nature of his purpose very clear to the heirs of what was promised, he confirmed it with an oath. God did this so that, by two unchangeable things in which it is impossible for God to lie, we who have fled to take hold of the hope offered to us may be greatly encouraged." The "two unchangeable things" are God's promise and His oath, which together encourage the heirs of the inheritance. The heirs have "fled to take hold of the hope." That is, our constant recourse in life is to the promises of God. This is in stark contrast to the disciples, who fled during the Savior's Passion because they had no hope (Mark 14:43–52).

Verse 19a: "We have this hope as an anchor for the soul, firm and secure." John Calvin has a beautiful comment on this image:

> *Certainly as long as we are pilgrims in this world we have no firm ground to stand on, but we are tossed about as if we were in the midst of the sea, and a stormy one at that. The devil never ceases from stirring up countless tempests which should at once capsize and submerge our ship if we do not cast our anchor far down in the depths.... There is this difference, that an anchor is cast down on the sea because there is solid ground at the bottom, but our hope rises and flies aloft because it finds nothing to stand on in this world. It cannot rely on created things, but finds rest in God alone.... The truth of God is a chain for binding us to himself, so that no distance of place and no darkness may hinder us from cleaving to him. When we are bound in this way to God, even though we have to contend with continual storms, we are safe from the danger of shipwreck. That is why he says that the anchor is sure and steadfast.*

In verses 19b–20 hope is personified: "It enters the inner sanctuary behind the curtain, where Jesus, who went before us, has entered on our behalf. He has become a high priest forever, in the order of Melchizedek." The inner sanctuary is the Holy of Holies, which only the high priest could enter on the Day of Atonement. Our hope enters the Holy of Holies because our hope is set on Jesus, our high priest (cf. Heb. 12:2). Every sermon should be Christocentric. This verse brings the previous verses to focus on Christ. In verse 20b the author moves beyond our pericope by introducing the discussion of Jesus as high priest (7:1–8:6). It also resumes the development of the argument that was interrupted at 5:11 in order to urge the Hebrews to spiritual maturity in the face of the temptation to lapse back into Judaism.

Sermon Starters

Central thought: Christians have an anchor for their life, hope in the promises of God.

Outline 1:   **Hope as an Anchor of the Soul**
  I. People need an anchor in life.
      A. At times of crisis (death, serious illness, etc.)
      B. At times that are "normal"
      C. A source of stability
 II. Christian hope: your anchor firm and secure
      A. Christian hope is not the fickle hope of the world.
      B. Christian hope is firm and secure because of God.
          1. Directed toward God
          2. Based on His promise confirmed by oath
III. Hope seen in the Anchor Cross
      A. Only an anchor to others, a cross of hope to us!
      B. Our hope is Christ.
          1. Christ died for us.
          2. He entered the Holy of Holies.
          3. Our hope follows Him to the very presence of God.
IV. "Which hope we have!"
      A. Uncertainty of those without hope
          1. Rabbi Jochanan
          2. Lobster fisherman's grave
      B. Our firm and secure anchor
          1. Dolly Pickett's grave
          2. Your hope!

Outline 2:   **"In the Sure and Certain Hope"**
  I. Introduction: The words of committal
 II. Sure and certain?
      A. Colloquial expressions of hope
      B. Uncertainty of salvation
III. Biblical hope is sure and certain.
      A. Like an anchor, today's symbol

B. Why it is sure and certain
   1. Basis of Christian life (Prov. 23:18)
   2. Makes life worth living (Lam. 3:18)
   3. God-centered (Ps. 42:11)
   4. Based on Jesus' resurrection (1 Peter 1:3)
IV. Our anchor of hope is as sure and certain as God Himself.
   A. God's promises to us
   B. God's confirming oath
   C. God's High Priest: Jesus
V. Hope is our constant recourse in life.
   A. Like Abraham
   B. Unlike the fleeing disciples
VI. Conclusion: Our stay in death
   A. Dolly Pickett's gravestone
   B. The hope is sure and certain!

Outline 3:   **At Sea, but Not Adrift**

I. Introduction: Life as a voyage
   A. Time of calm
   B. Times of storm and tempest
II. Adrift in storm and tempest
   A. Times of crisis (death, financial loss, etc.)
   B. Resultant insecurities
III. Our anchor: Christian hope
   A. Symbolism of the Anchor Cross
   B. Passages describing the security of the anchor of hope:
   1. Proverbs 23:18
   2. Lamentations 3:18
   3. Psalm 42:11
   4. 1 Peter 1:3
IV. How hope secures us in life
   A. It anchors us to God's good purposes (vv. 16–18).
   1. His promise
   2. His oath
   B. It follows Jesus (v. 20).
   1. The great High Priest
   2. Entered the Holy of Holies before us
V. Hope: Our anchor to use
   A. John Calvin on this text
   B. Negative example of disciples fleeing
   C. "In ev'ry high and stormy gale, my anchor holds within the veil" (*Lutheran Worship* 368:2).
VI. Conclusion: Now we are at sea, but not adrift!

Sermon: The Cross of Hope

Hebrews 6:13–20

Words change their meaning as time goes by and even ideas sometimes change their sense as surrounding circumstances change. Because this is true, things that once were plain become obscure over the course of time. That is in part what has given rise to so many new translations of the Scriptures in our day and age. Old translations needed a revision of vocabulary and phraseology in order to speak more plainly to people in our age.

But sometimes one is stuck with a word, so to speak. It cannot be interpreted simply by the use of a new word or phrase, but its strength has been taken away by changing cultures, eroded by the passage of time, or replaced by changing experiences of life as times change. Yet there it stands. And it needs to be dealt with.

We have three such instances in our text for this evening. The idea of the promise and/or the oath is one of them, and it stands at the very heart of the text. But none of us have really experienced the power of the word in its original setting when such things were taken very, very seriously. It meant something very different in its day from what we understand when we speak of a promise or an oath today. It is vital to realize this if we are to experience the power of the text.

The second word that lies in the core of the text is "hope." It, too, has undergone considerable transformation from the time when it was used in Hebrews. Its strength depends on understanding the promise and/or oath about which we were just speaking. If the meaning of this word is reduced to what we generally understand when we speak of "hope" in our day, we will lose the thrust of the text.

We can still picture the third strong image well, but it, too, carries a special sense that we must attempt to recapture if we want the text to be as lively as it was meant to be. That is the simple word "anchor." In the sea-dependent nations of Biblical times, an anchor had a symbolic meaning that we have lost to a large extent in our day when so much commerce is conducted by land or air.

When the strength of these words is restored to our text, we will find a strong assurance from God that His promises hold us anchored safely in and through Christ when the storms of life surround us and threaten to destroy us.

Promise/Oath

It is not unusual to hear promises made almost frivolously. "Come again soon," we are urged as we leave a friend's home. "I will. I promise," we respond, knowing very well that we will not be back anytime in the near future.

Oaths are made with equal casualness. "I swear to God that I saw a cat cross the road," we say to our wife as she challenges our nighttime vision.

Oaths and promises were taken much more seriously in the days when

Hebrews was written and in the days of Abraham, concerning whom the promise and oath were made. Even contracts were often executed simply by word of mouth in the presence of at least two witnesses or with one witness and an oath before God. A person's word was all that was necessary for most everyday kinds of transactions. A paperless society lived and did business quite differently from what we would consider proper and even legally necessary. Although written documents were executed on occasion, in general the spoken word was binding so long as it was properly witnessed. And even without a witness, a promise was still a very serious—almost sacred—word.

That is difficult to comprehend in a society where written contracts and deeds, notarized written agreements, and legal documents are vital to our business and personal activities. We scrutinize our written documents carefully, lest we be victimized by the fine print in which someone tries to put something over on us. But we must recognize that a mere spoken word was legally binding in the days of our text. The power of its message depends on our understanding this power of a spoken promise or oath.

That message leans on a promise God made to Abraham, the father of Israel and an honored forebear of the Christian faith. He left his native land under a special promise from God that he would father a great nation. The promise was repeated and embellished over the course of time. Finally, an oath was added to the promise after Abraham had showed his great trust in God by being willing to sacrifice his only son, the son of his old age, Isaac.

The writer points to this event: "When God made his promise to Abraham, since there was no one greater for him to swear by, he swore by himself, saying, 'I will surely bless you and give you many descendants.' . . . Men swear by someone greater than themselves, and the oath confirms what is said and puts an end to all argument. Because God wanted to make the unchanging nature of his purpose very clear to the heirs of what was promised, he confirmed it with an oath. God did this so that, by two unchangeable things in which it is impossible for God to lie, we who have fled to take hold of the hope offered to us may be greatly encouraged" (Heb. 6:13–18).

This whole passage depends on understanding that oaths required two witnesses or one witness and an "oath to God." The writer notes that "by two unchangeable things . . . we who have fled . . . may be greatly encouraged" (v. 18). Since God had nobody greater to whom He might appeal in making His oath to undergird His promise to Abraham, we are assured that we can depend on the original oath made by God. God staked His honor on what He promised Abraham, affirming in the oath His original promise that already in itself bound Him by honor to fulfill it.

Let's paraphrase it this way: "Do you think God can lie? Or is He bound to keep His word once He gives it?" And this line of reasoning is then drawn out as though still written large over the lives of all those who are of Abraham and the faith that has come through him, confirming the promise of God to Abraham by extension to all of his descendants. When God speaks, the result is as good as done, no matter how long it takes to get it done.

The people to whom the book of Hebrews is addressed seem to be wavering badly in the faith and the writer is trying to shore up their faith. He insists that God does not speak idly. So he points to God's faithfulness, by which He will always do what He says He will do even though one may see no immediate sign of its fulfillment. You can always trust that word implicitly, the writer insists. "And so after waiting patiently, Abraham received what was promised" (v. 15). That is the encouragement that lies under this strong emphasis on God's promise and/or oath.

Hope

The strong sense of an oath and promise that must necessarily be kept if God's honor is to be upheld governs the design of this text. It gives shape and form to the word "hope," another word that holds a central place for the readers.

It often amounts to little more than wishful thinking in our day. Sometimes it is a bit stronger—a yearning, a longing for something. When a man "hopes" a certain woman will marry him, he is saying that it is his heart's desire, but he is not certain that she will do so. The word has an element of tentativeness about it, perhaps even a very deep question about whether our hopes will ever really come true.

Biblical usage, however, handles the word in quite another way. It expresses certainty, confidence, assurance. "The hope of our salvation" is a Scriptural way of saying that our salvation is sure. We can rely on it. It is a certainty on which we can build the whole of life. It is far more than just wishful thinking. It is a confident assertion.

Such certainty is based on the promise of God to which we have already devoted so much attention. When the text speaks of "strong encouragement to seize the hope set before us," it is urging the readers to lay hold of a sure thing. God's promise is reinforced with an oath on His honor that, just as He cared for Abraham and kept all His promises to him, so also He will care for us.

The comfort of this hope is that it carries with it the assurance that God sees and knows your needs. His promises already tell you that He knows your need. He raises hope precisely because He sees the desperation with which all of us live so much of our lives.

To "hope in God" is to believe that He realizes how deeply the whole world is mired in the mud of sin with all its consequences. It is to recognize that even before you cry for help, God is on His way to free you from the situation in which you have become trapped and from which you cannot extricate yourselves. "Hope" is a trust that God's heart bleeds with the hurts and aches and pains of all who have become so deeply enmeshed in the fallenness of this broken world. A spider's web of sin holds us all fast, and only an outside agent can break us loose. "Hope" is not just wishing that someone would come to help you; it is the eye that already sees God on His way to free you. He comes to break you loose from the web that holds you, to remove the sting from your sin, to take away the victory the grave wants to claim when you die.

Hope is far more than merely building castles in the air, wishing that something or someone could or would change things. It is something on which you can count, in which you can trust with fullest certainty. As God once stood in the midst of the fiery serpents in the wilderness where Israel felt the threat of extinction, so also He stands in the midst of our warring madness today, in the midst of our economic muddling, in the midst of our diseases and our weaknesses, our worries and our fears. He stands with arms extended and with hope written large across His breast. He gathers us under the assurance that He will never leave us nor forsake us.

This promise is supported with an oath: "Because God wanted to make the unchanging nature of his purpose very clear to the heirs of what was promised, he confirmed it with an oath. God did this so that, by two unchangeable things in which it is impossible for God to lie, we who have fled to take hold of the hope offered to us might be greatly encouraged" (Heb. 6:17–18). Do the words not leap with strength now?

The oath that supports His promise is none less than the Word made flesh, enthroned on a cross, and crowned with thorns. When people ask how you dare to speak such hope into what seems such a hopeless world, you need do no more than point to the One who walks the way of humility and the way of suffering and sorrow, the Servant of God and the Servant of humankind. God has raised up hope in our midst through the life, suffering, death, and resurrection of our Lord Jesus Christ. He will not fail you if you place your hope in him. Can God lie? What He says, He does.

The Anchor

The anchor is the easiest of the three words we introduced earlier to describe physically. We have all seen pictures of anchors even if we have not actually handled one personally. You know it is a heavy item, usually equipped with some sort of hook to grab hold of the bed beneath the water to keep the ship from drifting when a stable mooring is necessary. It holds the boat in place when tides or storms threaten to drive it from its appointed place of rest.

In times of old the anchor was a symbol for anything that proved stable when everything around was being dashed to pieces. It described something that enabled a person to weather a storm swirling around him/her. Such usages are found even in philosophical treatises of the ancient world, when seafaring gave rise to many figures of speech.

The early Christians found great meaning and comfort in the Anchor Cross, displayed as our cross for this service. It identified and expressed a fundamental aspect of Christian faith. This form of the cross, used from early days of Christianity, was especially meaningful during the time of persecution before Christianity became legitimate under the rule of the Roman emperor Constantine. It was especially useful since Christians who could be killed for their faith could display it openly without fear. Non-Christians would see it as harmless, a common sign of the culture. With only slight modification, the anchor became a way of displaying the cross, and it was perceived by believers as a sign of hope and stability in very unsettled times so far as their own personal welfare was concerned. Perhaps it was already emerging as a primary Christian symbol when the writer of today's text said, "We have this hope as an anchor for the soul, firm and secure" (v. 19).

God's Promise: The Anchor of Hope in Your Life

In putting all these elements together, we find the inner kernel of how this text addresses you and me in the late 20th century. You have felt the storms of life beating on you, have you not? Who has escaped the winds of life's adversities? Who has not suffered sleepless nights of worry? Threatened health, financial concern, doubts and questions of faith, trembling in the very shadows of death—our own or that of a loved one—are all interconnected with the storms that threaten to blow you off your moorings, causing an aimless drift out onto the sea of life. The storms can come up so quickly and howl so fiercely that you hardly know which way to turn or where you can feel safe. Sometimes you may wonder whether the very foundations of the earth are shaking from the fury that rages around existence in the late 20th century.

The sign of the cross set before your eyes this evening is designed to bring a sense of stability into such troubled waters of life. The anchor does not stop the storm, which continues to rage mercilessly at times. But it establishes a place of safety for you when it is planted in the firm ground of God's promise, supported by the oath of Jesus' cross. Anchored, as it were, by that very cross of Christ, the faithfulness of God will always attach itself to you through this Man of the cross, into whose name you have been baptized. The Anchor Cross assures you that when the winds of adversity blow most strongly on you, you are safe in the loving care of Him whose Son gives you security even in the very jaws of death!

And the Anchor Cross does something else for you. It points you to the certainty of the harbor that lies beyond your sight. Even when you travel with favorable winds, the Anchor Cross still lies there in the boat of your life, assuring you that the journey has an end, a harbor toward which you are moving. It assures us that the tempestuous sea is not endless and that the Land of Promise lies beyond the horizon.

This is important on your journey, for hope is not only a way to stabilize life when the winds are against you; it is also a way of having a vision, a way of seeing through and beyond what is presently visible. It raises your eyes from the seemingly endless expanse of water that is our world to see with eyes of faith that there is a place to which you journey—a goal for your wandering, which seems to be without direction as you see nothing but water on every side. Therefore it helps to mold your life even while you are still traveling as it makes you aware that when you conclude the journey, the Father will greet you. He will hold out His arms and enfold you with love and joy, for His child will then have safely arrived in the final harbor.

If you know this, if you live by this hope, this confidence, this certainty, you will be both encouraged in your journey and stabilized in the storms of life because there is One who stands at the end of the journey waiting with open arms, scanning the sea and watching for the first sign of your approach. If you have a vision like that, you will find the journey worthwhile and will, even before the harbor is in sight, begin trembling with joy, conforming and configuring your life in anticipation of giving it over entirely to the One who awaits the time when you throw out your anchor in the final homecoming.

Maltese Cross—Regeneration

Sermon Study

Text: James 1:16–18
Passion Reading: Mark 14:53–65

Introduction

This week we worship at the Maltese Cross. It's name comes from Malta, a small island situated between Sicily and Africa in the Mediterranean. The Knights of St. John were banished there in the Middle Ages. The cross is sometimes called the "Regeneration Cross" because its eight points symbolize the eight beatitudes that describe the blessed life of the regenerate. Regeneration is what this and every cross of Lent is all about.

Nathaniel Hawthorne's short story "The Birthmark" tells where human attempts at regeneration will lead. A certain scientist, known the world over for his discoveries, won the hand of a beautiful and much courted woman named Georgiana. The scientist, Aylmer by name, loved his wife dearly but became increasingly obsessed with the only blemish to Georgiana's beauty, a birthmark that looked like a tiny hand on her cheek. Aylmer's growing obsession so disturbed the peace of the marriage that Georgiana finally consented to surgery. Aylmer, a great and qualified authority, confident that he could remove the birthmark surgically, performed the operation. The shocking result: Georgiana died! This human attempt at perfection ended in failure. Hawthorne says those failures are "the sad confession and continual exemplification of the shortcomings of the composite man, the spirit burdened with clay and working in matter, and of the despair that assails the higher nature at finding itself so miserably thwarted by the earthy part."

The Maltese Cross directs us to the divine work of regeneration. St. Paul saw the problem as did Hawthorne, but Paul gives the solution: "What a wretched man I am! Who will rescue me from this body of death? Thanks be to God—through Jesus Christ our Lord!" (Rom. 7:24–25). Jesus, whose cross makes regeneration possible, told Nicodemus: "I tell you the truth, no one can enter the kingdom of God unless he is born of water and the Spirit" (John 3:5). James puts it this way in the text for this week:

> *Don't be deceived, my dear brothers. Every*
> *good and perfect gift is from above, coming*
> *down from the Father of the heavenly lights,*
> *who does not change like shifting shadows.*
> *He chose to give us birth through the word of*
> *truth, that we might be a kind of firstfruits*
> *of all he created. (James 1:16–18)*

Background: The Regeneration of James

The full details of James's rebirth must be an interesting story. We can only speculate about it on the basis of New Testament evidence. The New Testament tells of at least three men named James: a son of Zebedee, a son of Alphaeus, and James the brother of Jesus. This last James is the author of this week's text and an interesting case study in regeneration. That he was actually Jesus' brother, born to Mary and Joseph sometime after the virgin birth of the Savior, seems evident. Paul wrote of his trip to Jerusalem: "I saw none of the other apostles—only James, the Lord's brother" (Gal. 1:19). Jude 1 says "Jude, a servant of Jesus Christ and a brother of James." This last passage indicates that there were more brothers, and Matthew 13:55 provides the confirmation: "Isn't this the carpenter's son? Isn't his mother's name Mary, and aren't his brothers James, Joseph, Simon, and Judas?"

Since he came from such a family, you would expect James to be a life-long saint! The evidence, though not conclusive, suggests that he was not. He is not mentioned among the close disciples of Jesus and was probably not part of the larger circles, such as the 70. A passage in Matthew lets us conjecture that James and the rest of the family kept at a distance from Jesus' ministry. "Someone told him [Jesus], 'Your mother and brothers are standing outside, wanting to speak with you.' He replied to him, 'Who is my mother, and who are my brothers?' Pointing to his disciples, he said, 'Here are my mother and my brothers. For whoever does the will of my Father in heaven is my brother and sister and mother' " (12:47–50). James was so close to the Savior and yet so far away.

But God gave him the new birth. In Acts we find that James is a leader of the early church. When an angel effects Peter's escape from prison, Peter says "Tell James and the brothers about this" (Acts 12:17). James appears later as the president of the apostolic council that addressed the question of Gentiles in the church. After Peter, Paul, and Barnabas had related their experiences with the Gentile mission, James gave his judgment. It was put into writing and sent to the believers at Antioch (Acts 15:13–29).

There's no doubt that James was reborn, but the circumstances of the conversion are uncertain. A popular suggestion comes from 1 Corinthians 15:7: "Then he [the resurrected Lord] appeared to James." This appearance, many think, was James's "Damascus Road" experience. Whether it happened at that time or earlier is intriguing but of minor importance compared to the fact that it did happen. God gave him the new birth that his "brother" had talked about years before. Had it not been for the fact that God "chose to give us birth through the word of truth" (James 1:18), James would have ended up no different than the characters in this week's passion reading (Mark 14:53–65). Annas, Caiaphas, the soldiers who struck and spit at Jesus, and the members of the Sanhedrin were unregenerate, resisting new birth through the word of truth. But James was different. He became a "kind of firstfruits of all [God] created" because of the divine work of regeneration.

Context: Blessed is the One Who Does Not Forget What He Has Heard

The eight points of the Maltese Cross represent the eight beatitudes, eight blessings from Christ on those who live as God's covenant people. James writes to Christians who are beginning to forget how God wants His reborn people to live. They are grumbling when confronted by trials and temptations (1:2–15) to such an extent that their commitment is wavering (1:6). They are becoming cliquish (2:1–13), quick with the tongue (1:26; 3:1–12), proud, envious, and ambitious (3:13–18). They were overly impressed by the rich and the influential, perhaps thinking that these people could further the church's cause more than the poor (5:1–6). There is a hint in the letter that the Christians to whom James writes looked on these sins as part of the exercise of true religion (3:15). James compares their situation to that of a corpse: "As the body without the spirit is dead, so faith without deeds is dead" (2:26). To shift the imagery, they are like the Maltese Cross without its eight points. James reminds his readers that the regenerate life is both faith and action born of the word. "The man who looks intently into the perfect law that gives freedom, and continues to do this, not forgetting what he has heard, but doing it—he will be blessed in what he does" (1:25).

Jesus spoke His beatitudes in a similar context: The Pharisees had separated faith and works. Whereas James's readers were holding faith without works, the Pharisees had actions but no faith. They prayed, went to the Temple, fasted, aided the poor, did mission work, and on and on—pious deeds that would have been acceptable to God if they had come from faith. But Jesus condemned their religious deeds because they did not come from a repentant heart. "On the outside you appear to people as righteous but on the inside you are full of hypocrisy and wickedness" (Matt. 23:28). The beatitudes are a gentle reminder from Jesus to His own disciples that their life should proceed from faith. The poor in spirit, those who mourn, the meek, those who hunger and thirst for righteousness, the merciful, the pure in heart—these are the marks of a repentant spirit, "a broken and contrite heart" (Ps. 51:17), which are acceptable to God and constitute a blessed life. People who live by the word of the cross are blessed.

Whether it be the Pharisees or James's readers, the basic problem, the separation of faith and action, was the same for both. They had taken their eyes from God and were more intent on their own situations. So James directs them back to God, the source of rebirth and Christian life. God gives wisdom, not man, and God gives "generously to all without finding fault" (James 1:5). He promises the crown of life to those who love Him, and so we should view temptation as a test of faith rather than an occasion to be self-righteous toward others, including God (1:12; 5:9). He has given the kingdom to those who love Him rather than to the rich (2:5). Christians, therefore, should not show favoritism any more than Jesus did during His ministry. God makes a person righteous through faith, and so people should not take comfort merely in their external association with the church (v.

23). Again and again, James takes his hearers back to God's action and never tires of promising blessing to those who hear and do the Word. This week's sermon does just that.

Text: James 1:16–18

Verse 16: "Don't be deceived, my dear brothers." The address to "brothers" is a reference to Christians. Although this letter has been faulted for its lack of explicit Gospel formulations, the Gospel is very much present and the use of "brothers" reminds us that James is addressing the regenerate. "Deceived" translates the Greek word from which the English "planet" is derived. Unlike the stars, which appear to be fixed in the heavens, the planets wander (cf. James 5:19; Jude 13). James draws out the comparison in the next verse.

Verse 17: "Every good and perfect gift is from above, coming down from the Father of the heavenly lights, who does not change like shifting shadows." "Every good and perfect gift" is probably a hendiadys. The adjectives leave no room for human boasting, for the Father is the source of all (cf. 1:5). "Perfect" is one of James's favorite words, indicating a holiness that was lacking in his readers' lives (cf. 1:4, 17, 25; 2:22; 3:2). "From above" and "down" suggest gift rather than merit (cf. "Our Father, who art in heaven"; John 3:3,7). The Father is described with light imagery. Unlike the lights of the sky which are of varying brightness, the Father is constant. "God is light; in him there is no darkness at all" (1 John 1:5). "I the Lord do not change" (Mal. 3:6).

Verse 18: James 1:15 described a process of conception and birth with bad consequences: "Then, after desire has conceived, it gives birth to sin; and sin, when it is full-grown, gives birth to death." Compare the result of Aylmer's desire in "The Birthmark"—death! Now in verse 18 James presents a welcome contrast. "He chose to give us birth through the word of truth, that we might be a kind of firstfruits of all he created." Regeneration is a result of God's will, not ours. He accomplished our birth "through the word of truth." Peter also sees regeneration through the Word: "You have been born again, not of perishable seed, but of imperishable, through the living and enduring word of God" (1 Peter 1:23; cf. also 1 Cor. 4:15). Rabbi Jose ben Zimra said in the third century that the person who converts a Gentile "is as if he created him." "That we might be" is probably a purpose clause. Regeneration sets us on the road of good works. "A kind of" softens the metaphor of firstfruits. Jesus had described Christians as salt and light in society (Matt. 5:13–16). Paul wrote: "For it is by grace you have been saved, through faith—and this not from yourselves, it is the gift of God—not by works, so that no one can boast. For we are God's workmanship, created in Christ Jesus to do good works, which God prepared in advance for us to do" (Eph. 2:8–10). Here we must caution the preacher outlining his sermon: Keep the focus on God's gift of regeneration, and do not let the necessary works of sanctification displace the central truth that God justifies and gives new birth. Paul and James have the right perspective, but pastors sometimes become so frustrated by the lives of their members that sanctification in the narrow sense becomes the chief article of their ministry. Compare the Formula of Concord, Art. II: "Holy Scriptures ascribe conversion, faith in Christ, regeneration, renewal, and everything that belongs to its real beginning and completion in no way to the human powers of the natural free will … but altogether and alone to the divine operation and the Holy Spirit" (FC SD ii 25; The Book of Concord, trans. and ed. Theodore G. Tappert [St. Louis: Concordia Publishing House, 1959], p. 526).

Sermon Starters

Central thought: Only God gives rebirth to a blessed life.

Outline 1:   **Birthmarks of the Blessed**
  I. Introduction
    A. "You must be born again" (John 3:7).
    B. The Maltese Cross, the cross of regeneration
 II. We cannot regenerate ourselves.
    A. "The Birthmark" by Hawthorne: An attempt to produce the perfect person ends in death.
    B. Human attempts at regeneration
       1. Pharisees: Religious works
       2. James's readers: Dead orthodoxy
    C. Result: Death (cf. James 1:15)
III. God alone gives new birth.
    A. James 1:18
    B. God wills our rebirth.
    C. God does it through the word of truth.
 IV. Birthmarks of the blessed
    A. Rebirth shows.
    B. The eight points of the Maltese Cross represent the beatitudes, the marks of the blessed.
    C. Born again? Let it show!

Outline 2:   **Points of the Cross**
  I. Introduction: Maltese Cross
    A. The cross symbolizes regeneration.
    B. The points symbolize the beatitudes, the life of the blessed.
 II. Without rebirth, life is pointless.
    A. Human attempts at regeneration
       1. Pharisees: Religious works
       2. James's hearers: Dead orthodoxy
    B. Result: Death (cf. James 1:15)
III. James: One reborn life
    A. James before rebirth
    B. The word of truth gave James new birth.
    C. Reborn, productive James
 IV. You're reborn!

A. God wills and accomplishes your regeneration.

B. "The Holy Ghost has called me by the Gospel."

C. Center of rebirth: The cross of Christ

V. Reborn, your life has points.

A. The points of Maltese Cross represent the beatitutes, the marks of the blessed.

B. Your life has points: You're reborn to be productive.

Outline 3:   **God Makes It Work!**

I. Introduction

A. If it works, don't fix it.

B. What do you do when it doesn't work, when a person is not living God's life?

II. It didn't work for the Jewish leadership.

A. Annas, Caiaphas, and their cohorts condemned Jesus (Passion reading).

B. Though religious leaders, they could not do God's will but could only work death (cf. James 1:15).

C. "I believe that I cannot by my own reason or strength believe in Jesus Christ my Lord."

III. When it doesn't work: New birth needed!

A. "But the Holy Ghost has called me by the Gospel."

B. James 1:18

C. God alone wills and gives us the needed new birth.

IV. God makes His word work in your life.

A. Productive life of the regenerate

B. "Firstfruits of all he created" (James 1:18)

V. Conclusion: The Maltese Cross

A. The cross symbolizes the new birth God gives us.

B. The eight points symbolize the beatitudes, our productive lives.

C. Let God's Word work in your life!

Sermon: The Cross of Regeneration

James 1:16–18

Magicians astonish us as their sleight of hand tricks us. Mannequins startle us as we think a real person stands before us. Statistics say whatever someone chooses, depending on which set of figures a person decides to manipulate. Can anything in life be trusted? It seems that deceptions abound!

The Deceptions of Life

Although we are suspicious about appearances like those we have just mentioned, our age leads us to believe strongly in what can be seen and "proved" scientifically. Granted that we theorize about a lot of things, we nevertheless look for solid evidence that our eyes, ears, and reason find beyond dispute for the theories that we can trust. That is how we "know" things—by seeing them, feeling them, and understanding them. It is all too easy to forget how quickly and easily our eyes can be deceived.

It is the same with our ears. So many things fill them from so many sources that we hardly know what to believe. Ideas are multiplied endlessly and broadcast widely through every conceivable medium. One cannot believe everything one hears, for many things are contradictory, and others simply seem incredible in themselves. Precisely because of this we often construct our own ideas out of bits and pieces of this and that, all being joined together into some way of understanding life that seems to make sense—at least to us.

Our minds are supposedly rational, but even great minds see the same things and think entirely different thoughts about them. How are we to sort through everything and make sense out of it? You surely have experienced occasions when your rational mind lost all contact with reality in a moment of fear or great stress, have you not? It is something like that when our minds are fed such a variety of things through the eye and the ear. When we must make sense out of this endless array of ideas we just rearrange everything, and good teachings and sound understandings become mixed with bizarre ideas and strange notions. We hardly realize it is happening.

All this affects our hearts very subtly but in a very real way. Imaginings of every sort send our lives in many different directions all at once. We know we should provide for the future, but there is grave question about whether there will be a future; we should love our neighbor, but needs are so great, and there are so many who take advantage of us that we don't know how to love; we want to do good, but our best efforts seem to turn to dust in our hands. We don't know which way to turn or what to do, so our heart turns inward. We live only for ourselves and hope we don't get hurt too badly so that we can enjoy a reasonably happy lifetime before returning to dust. And we settle for that.

This is what Luther meant when he described "the devil, the world, and our flesh" having at us night and day from every imaginable angle of life. Voices from outside urge us to see and listen to things that are not of God. The world opens its arms to reenforce our sight and hearing with the idea that true security lies in what the world can offer, and our flesh buys into it hook, line, and sinker.

All of this seems magnified in our day. We are bombarded with reassurances that what pleases our senses surely is what we need for security and happiness. One cannot effectively escape this insistent voice urging us to enjoy life in the way that our culture dictates.

In the face of all this, our text for today speaks out of a context of "temptation." It is a bridge toward understanding what makes a godly life. James warns us, "Don't be deceived" (1:16), which is what "temptation" is all about. The Greek word for "deceived" has a wide variety of interrelated ideas imbedded within it. It can mean "to lead astray," "to vacillate," "absence of a goal," "to be mistaken," "aimless conduct," or "entanglement."

So it involves more than "Don't let the wool be pulled over your eyes."

It can mean "Don't let wrong things lead you astray," or "Don't be shiftless, vacillating back and forth about what is good and doing it," or "Don't go through life without a goal, letting this and that pull you every which way," or "Don't be mistaken about what life is all about," or "Don't get entangled with things that will undo your life," or "Don't get caught up in doing just any old thing with your life." There are plenty of temptations or deceits that will lead you in wrong directions. Don't let them mislead you, James is saying, for their tug at your heartstrings is great.

The Truth of Eternity

Over against this deceit, James points to what endures and provides stability amidst our wavering. He reminds us of the ground for a godly life even when surrounded by temptation. One must have new and different eyes and ears for this entirely different word. It speaks and gives a vision quite other than the world gives. And it will create another kind of mindset, opening wholly contrasting possibilities for living from anything available purely on the basis of this world's level of existence. It is nothing short of a "rebirth," a "regeneration" of everything from the way we see and hear to how we live.

This life is only available "from above," James tells us, "coming down from the Father of the heavenly lights, who does not change like shifting shadows" (v. 17). The imagery is born of a very old way of seeing the heavens. The ancients looked to the heavens as a place where things were "established" compared to the changing nature of this earth. Although the stars "swing around" by the times of the year, there is still a "fixedness" about them. One can depend on the North Star and the constellations holding their place. Seafarers could know where they were, and lost travelers could regain their direction because the heavens could be trusted. They were the chart and compass of people in ancient times.

That is how God is, James tells us. He alone can chart your life and direct your path in safe ways, guiding you home from your wanderings. From Him comes "every good and perfect gift." Over against what the world offers you, all of which perishes and easily misleads you completely if you use these things as your goal and security, God comes down from above and becomes your shield from danger, your compass in your wanderings, and your hope (as we noted last week) in the storms of life.

James's message is a bridge between the little teaching on temptations, introduced earlier ("Blessed is the man who perseveres under trial," v. 12) and an exhortation to the godly life that will go on to say, "My dear brothers, take note of this: Everyone should be quick to listen, slow to speak, and slow to become angry" (v. 19). James instructs us as he moves from the one topic to the other to keep in mind what deceitfulness surrounds us in our seeing, hearing, and experiencing on the purely human level. He encourages us to look for guidance and stability to the Giver of every good and perfect gift, who "does not change like shifting shadows" (v. 17).

To confirm us in this confidence he adds, "He chose to give us birth through the word of truth, that we might be a kind of firstfruits of all he created" (v. 18). We must remember that he addresses these words to "dear brothers." These are not people who still live in darkness, for they have already received that perfect gift from the Father of light by which they have been changed. James points again to the "word of truth" by which God chose to "give us birth." He has given us a new birth, regenerated us, given us new eyes and ears and hearts and lives.

This same word continues to be necessary because deceitful temptations surround us. In this word we are to live and move and have our being, for in it God will keep us stable and on target, headed for the goal He has established, and kept on the way of God.

This "word of truth" by which we are brought forth to "be a kind of firstfruits of all he created" is more than a spoken or written word. It has become flesh and lived and died among us as our Brother. He, too, knew temptation like us. We hear Him cry out from the intensity of His temptation in the Garden of Gethsemane. His words from the cross about God-forsakenness tear at our hearts as He speaks of His temptation to think that God had led Him, literally, on a dead-end path. Psalm 22, from which His words came, however, is at heart a cry of deep-seated faith. So this Brother of ours on the cross cries out in temptation but with yet unwavering faith that His God-forsakenness is not without hope. He overcomes our human plight by enduring what we endure in our stead and for our salvation.

So He went into the very grave for which we are all headed. This is the "word of truth" that, in fleshly form, gives us confidence that the Word spoken by God and in behalf of God is not an empty word. His taking up our death is, in fact, the last word to which we must look when we are tempted to think that God has forsaken us and left us to our own devices. The world shouts in a deafening roar to us when we are crucified with burdens and distresses, "Come down now from the cross, and we will believe in God. You trust in God; let God deliver you now, if He desires you." But we remember the company we keep. It is so tempting to put away faith when these taunting voices surround us. But they are the same voices that came to Jesus on the cross. They come now to us in our trouble—tempting voices, pointing deceivingly to visions of life without a cross, of pleasure without pain, of a life lived only in self-fulfillment without any of the dimensions God makes available to us "from above." What counts is what we see and feel, the voices taunt. And they are powerful voices.

Then there is only one place to look: to the cross where you join yourself to a Brother whose trust that God's presence even in this awful hour would still "give us birth . . . that we might be a kind of firstfruits of his creation." The firstfruit of resurrection then joins itself to your life, making it, in turn, a firstfruit of new life on earth.

The Crossover from God's Truth to Our Life

Faith is the word that points to that connection. It is where what happened "then and there" becomes the "here and now" for you.

On the cross God offers you truth that comes from the Father of all truth. He calls your ear from all other words to his Word alone. He calls your eyes from that limited vision of this world to what is revealed from above. He calls your mind and heart and life from the smallness of this world's thinking and living to a way that is as large as the very heart of God.

The form of the cross that holds our attention this evening—the Maltese Cross—speaks to this. It is said to have been created with a strong accent on its eight points as symbols of the eight beatitudes. It is called the "Regeneration Cross" sometimes on this account. For regeneration is not simply something that happens in a moment and then stops. To be born is a major event, but it is a birth to living. Stillborn children are buried immediately. Rebirth gives rise not only to new ways of seeing and hearing but also to a new way of life. And the beatitudes speak of the blessedness of life that is grounded in God. Blessed are the poor in spirit, those who mourn, the meek, those who hunger and thirst for righteousness, the merciful, the pure in heart, the peacemakers, those persecuted for righteousness' sake. These "blessed ones" are people of the new birth, the remaking of life into a "gift from above" to the world, the brothers and sisters of James.

Hard though it may be to imagine, *you* are God's gift to the world. Born again in the waters of Baptism, claimed by God "from above" and given back to the world as His child, living in the midst of and through temptation, forgiven and re-created daily—you are given in the name of Christ to the world. Luther puts it this way, speaking of the continuing power of our baptism: "The old person daily drowns and dies and a new person daily comes forth and arises." You, with your sins and the deceits of the world clinging to you, are daily swallowed up in the jaws of Jesus' death, where your sins are forgiven so that you can daily begin anew, given over and over to the world every day in the name of Christ. That is what happens when "the Father of the heavenly lights, who does not change like shifting shadows," visits you with his "good and perfect gift ... from above" and gives you "birth through the word of truth, that we might be a kind of firstfruits of all he created."

This is what Luther means when he speaks of our redeemed position as one in which we are "to live under Him in His kingdom and serve Him in everlasting righteousness, innocence, and blessedness."

It is to this that you are pointed by eight points of the Maltese Cross held before your eyes this evening. You are the children of God, given birth from above in the the womb of the cross to go forth in the name of God as those hungering and thirsting after righteousness, as the merciful, the pure in heart, the peacemakers of the earth.

Be what you are, the blessed of the earth, so that the earth through you might be blessedly reborn.

Week of Lent 4

Greek Cross—Suffering

Sermon Study

Text: 1 Peter 2:21–25
Passion Reading: John 19:18–42

Introduction

Lenten services can be sleepy times. Pastor and parishioners have worked all day long. Warming temperatures encourage outdoor activity—a great relief from cabin fever but also tiring after winter's hibernation indoors. What pastor has not sympathized with the nodding heads of listeners as he preached the evening service? The theme for this service should be so provocative that all will listen attentively. Thomas Sheppard's verse states the theme succinctly:

> *Must Jesus bear His cross alone*
> *And all the world go free?*
> *No, there's a cross for everyone*
> *And there's a cross for me!*

St. Peter puts it this way in the sermon text: "Christ suffered for you, leaving you an example, that you should follow in his steps" (1 Peter 2:21). Christians are called to suffer? That's not the message our people absorb day in and day out. Television shows depict people solving monumental problems in 30 or 60 minutes. Drugs deaden pain. Healthy diets and exercise programs promise happy lives. Lawyers stand ready to redress the slightest wrong. "You are called to follow Christ and suffer." Preach that effectively and no head will nod!

The Greek Cross presents the contradiction between the world's inclination for ease and the call of God to suffer. Its four arms of equal length come from the Greek love of symmetry, their love for beauty even in an instrument of torture like the cross. Yet the disquieting message of the cross cannot be concealed even by the Greeks. It is always first and foremost a reminder of the way our redemption was accomplished—by the wounds of Christ. Thus the Greek Cross is often used on the altar in a series of five Greek Crosses to call to the worshiper's mind the five wounds of the Savior. His suffering is the paradigm for the unjust suffering of Christians today. All that we regard as beauty, all the rationalizations of the modern world, cannot remove the cross from life. "Christ suffered for you, leaving you an example, that you should follow in his steps."

Background: Peter and Jesus on Suffering

The vocation of suffering is always hard to accept. Peter, the author of this week's sermon text, struggled against suffering. His eventual turnabout from revulsion to joy in suffering provides an excellent background to the text. Peter and the other disciples heard Jesus predict his passion at Caesarea Philippi. "Jesus began to explain to his disciples that he must go to Jerusalem and suffer many things at the hands of the elders, chief priests and teachers of the law, and that he must be killed and on the third day be raised to life" (Matt. 16:21; cf. Mark 8:31; Luke 9:22). Perhaps because he was the spokesman for the Twelve—certainly because of his impetuosity—Peter expressed his horror: "Never, Lord! This shall never happen to you!" (Matt. 16:22). Peter's reaction was caused not only by his affection for Jesus (Who wants to see a friend suffer?) but also by some popular but bad theology.

The Pharisees were the most influential group within first-century Judaism. They had about 6,000 members, who were associated with the synagogues throughout Israel. They were waiting for the Messiah, which was all well and good, but they were not expecting a Messiah whose career would end at the cross. The Psalms of Solomon, apocryphal writings from the first and second centuries before Christ, describe the triumphant Messiah that the Pharisees were telling Israelities to expect.

> *All nations shall be in fear before him, for*
> *he will smite the earth with the word of his*
> *mouth forever. . . . He will rebuke rulers, and*
> *remove sinners by the might of his word;*
> *and relying upon his God, throughout his*
> *days he will not stumble; for God will make*
> *him mighty by means of his holy spirit. . . .*
> *And the blessing of the Lord will be with*
> *him; he will be strong and stumble not; his*
> *hope will be in the Lord; who then can pre-*
> *vail against him? (Psalms of Solomon*
> *17:38–44)*

Although Peter was not a Pharisee, he lived near the synagogue at Capernaum and often heard this kind of talk about the coming Messiah. At Caesarea Philippi Peter had confessed that Jesus is the Christ, a confession that Jesus warmly accepted (Matt. 16:16–17; cf. 11:25–26). But it appears to Peter that Jesus is not fully acquainted with the job description of the Messiah. The Messiah should not suffer, especially at the hands of religious authorities. No wonder he reacted as he did!

Jesus chose to be very firm in handling Peter's objection to the cross. "Get behind me, Satan! You are a stumbling block to me; you do not have in mind the things of God, but the things of men" (16:23; cf. Mark 8:33). That rebuke is followed by the positive assertion that disciples of Jesus deny themselves and carry the cross (Matt. 16:24–28; Mark 8:34–38; Luke 9:23–27). Peter and his friends must have been perplexed by the whole conversation. They would hear it again and still not understand (Mark 9:31–32). And when Jesus had been crucified and raised, Peter and the disciples were still not done with the theme of suffering. Jesus told Peter, " 'Feed my sheep. I tell you the truth, when you were younger you dressed yourself and went where you wanted; but when you are old you will stretch out your hands, and someone else will dress you and lead you where you do not want to go.' Jesus said this to indicate the kind of death by which Peter would glorify God. Then he said to him, 'Follow me!' " (John 21:18–19). That's what this week's service is about: A suffering Christ, who bids us follow Him into suffering.

Context: 1 Peter

The sermon text indicates that Peter did come around. Writing to suffering Christians in the central and northern provinces of Asia Minor, he tells them that their temporary griefs should be suffused with a joyous hope.

> *Praise be to the God and Father of our Lord*
> *Jesus Christ! In his great mercy he has given*
> *us new birth into a living hope through the*
> *resurrection of Jesus Christ from the dead,*
> *and into an inheritance that can never per-*
> *ish, spoil, or fade—kept in heaven for you,*
> *who through faith are shielded by God's*
> *power until the coming of the salvation that*
> *is ready to be revealed in the last time. In*
> *this you greatly rejoice, though now for a lit-*
> *tle while you may have had to suffer grief in*
> *all kinds of trials. (1 Peter 1:3–6)*

What suffering these Christians were experiencing is uncertain. Conservative scholarship accepts the epistle as genuinely Petrine and suggests a date around A.D. 64, the year of the fire at Rome that Nero blamed on the Christians. Nero did not begin a formal persecution of Christians throughout the whole empire, but their alleged guilt at Rome must have endangered the safety of Christians in the provinces. The suspicions and gossip of their pagan neighbors must have been intensified by the fact that many Christians came from the lower class. The middle of the letter is directed to aliens and strangers (2:11–12), slaves (2:13–25), and wives (3:1–6). Thus the exhortation to slaves to suffer is especially loaded. Not only are they looked down on as lower class elements in society, but they have compounded their "guilt" by confessing the name of Christ. Like it or not, these Christians are carrying the cross, and it is not pretty.

Text: 1 Peter 2:21–25

> *To this you were called, because Christ suf-*
> *fered for you, leaving you an example, that*
> *you should follow in his steps. "He commit-*
> *ted no sin, and no deceit was found in his*
> *mouth." When they hurled their insults at*
> *him, he did not retaliate; when he suffered,*
> *he made no threats. Instead, he entrusted*
> *himself to him who judges justly. He himself*

bore our sins in his body on the tree, so that
we might die to sins and live for righteous-
ness; by his wounds you have been healed.
For you were like sheep going astray, but
now you have returned to the Shepherd and
Overseer of your souls.

Verse 21: "To this you were called, because Christ suffered for you, leaving you an example, that you should follow in his steps." "This" is "patient endurance when suffering unjustly" (Edward G. Selwyn, The First Epistle of St. Peter). "Called" is a theme throughout the letter. In verse 9, Peter says that his readers have been called "out of darkness" into God's "wonderful light." God's call promises them a glorious future: "The God of all grace, who called you to his eternal glory in Christ, after you have suffered a little while, will himself restore you and make you strong" (5:10). In 3:9 he speaks of that coming glory in terms of the heavenly inheritance: "To this you were called so that you may inherit a blessing" (cf. 1:4). Therefore, the present passage is a reminder to these afflicted people that they have status with God, even though their neighbors are laying a cross on them. "Christ suffered for you." Jesus is not just a model of suffering; He is the Savior, who suffered on our behalf. This is a statement of pure Gospel that Peter will amplify in the next verses. Note that Christ's sacrificial suffering is the basis of the Christian's vocation of suffering. Peter must have a very good reason for exhorting people to accept their suffering, and that reason is the sacrifice of Jesus Christ: "Leaving you an example, that you should follow in his steps." The Greek word suggests a stencil, such as children might use to learn how to write. Jesus' suffering provides the pattern that teaches us how to conduct ourselves during our own times of suffering.

Verse 22: "He committed no sin, and no deceit was found in his mouth." Peter quotes Isaiah 53:9 to give specifics on suffering. The person who suffers unjustly should guard his tongue. If a Christian is suffering because of his allegiance to Jesus, he may be unable or unwilling to retaliate with physical force against those who cause him harm. But how tempting to mutter a curse against the oppressors, how easy to promise revenge! Jesus did not, and He leaves us an example of suffering quietly for the faith.

Verse 23: "When they hurled their insults at him, he did not retaliate; when he suffered he made no threats. Instead, he entrusted himself to him who judges justly." Someone will ask "What should I do when suffering?" In America there are legal procedures that can be used for protection against some causes of unjust suffering. Peter's hearers did not have the same blessings of democracy and so are told to entrust their righteous cause to the heavenly Father. The Father who will judge was mentioned in 1:17: "Since you call on a Father who judges each man's work impartially, live your lives as strangers here in reverent fear." In 4:5 Peter promises that those who lead dissolute lives "will have to give account to him who is ready to judge the living and the dead." The problem that arises when a suffering person retaliates with a curse is that the sufferer is usurping God's right to judge.

James 4:12: "There is only one Lawgiver and Judge, the one who is able to save and destroy. But you—who are you to judge your neighbor?"

Upon your lips, then, lay your hand,
And trust his guiding love;
Then like a rock your peace shall stand
Here and in heaven above. (LW 424:7)

Verse 24: "He himself bore our sins in his body on the tree, so that we might die to sins and live for righteousness; by his wounds you have been healed." The first and last clauses of the verse are again taken from Isaiah 53. The use of "tree" for the cross is common. It was sometimes used for wooden stocks, gallows, clubs, and the like, usually suggesting criminality. The sufferer in this case is criminal only because He bears our sins. "He himself bore our sins" suggests the Old Testament priest, who brought the sacrificial victim and laid it on the altar (Lev. 14:20; Heb. 9:28). This Christ is not only a model but a Savior for sinners. The Passion reading for this Lenten service describes the Savior's time on the cross. Crucifixion was the Roman mode of execution. The condemned was stripped of his clothes, a practice that heightened the psychological element of the torture. Fastened to the cross by nails driven through the hands or wrists, the victim died slowly through hunger, thirst, fatique, and cramped muscles (cf. Luke 24:39). We can analyze the physical and emotional anguish of His death. We can depict it in art. We can understand the Greek's attempt to beautify the cross. But neither art nor words can convey the magnitude of His sacrifice for us. The meaning of the cross is so important to Peter. He gives little of the details, but makes the result clear. Dead to sin, we now live for righteousness even in times when we, too, suffer. Righteousness, a favorite concept of Paul, is not uncommon to Peter (2:23, 24; 3:12, 14, 18; 4:18).

Verse 25: "For you were like sheep going astray, but now you have returned to the Shepherd and Overseer of your souls." Again Isaiah 53 is used. Peter is fond of the imagery of sheep and shepherds. Not only were they common in the region around Capernaum, but Jesus impressed the image on Peter when He reinstated him (John 21). The word for "going astray" is the source of our English word "planet." Unlike the stars, the planets seem to wander in the heavens. Peter's recipients had wandered but now have a new and definite course laid out for them: following in Christ's steps (cf. v. 21). "Shepherd and Overseer" is a hendiadys. "Souls" refers to the whole person, not to a Platonic concept of soul. In the Shepherd's fold there is comfort and assurance for suffering sheep.

Sermon Starters

Central thought: The cross of Christ calls us to bear our own crosses.

Outline 1:   **"Drawn to the Cross"**
 I. Why are you drawn to the cross?
    A. Is it for its beauty?
    B. The Greeks beautified their cross.
 II. We are drawn to the cross because that is where Christ suffered for us.
    A. His wounds were the sacrifice for our sin.
    B. His suffering was great (cf. Passion reading).
 III. We are drawn each day to the cross.
    A. In our devotion
    B. To bear our own crosses
       1. Caused by our faith
       2. Our vocation
 IV. We are drawn to the cross by the beauty of forgiveness.

Outline 2:   **How Many Crosses?**
 I. The Greek Cross
    A. Background
    B. In a series of five for the five wounds of Christ
 II. How many crosses in your life?
    A. Various crosses
    B. Crosses due to Christian confession
    C. Called to patient endurance under these crosses
 III. The cross that counts the most
    A. His five wounds, the sacrifice for our sin
    B. His cross (cf. Passion reading)
 IV. How many crosses? The number of crosses in you life is insignificant
    because of His cross.

Outline 3:   **A Beautiful Cross to the Eye of Faith**
 I. Beauty is in the eyes of the beholders.
    A. You bear crosses because you are Christian.
    B. Did you ever consider them beautiful?
 II. Is Christ's cross beautiful?
    A. The Greeks tried to make it so.
    B. It remains an instrument of suffering.
       1. Death by crucifixion
       2. Jesus' great sorrow (cf. Passion reading)
    C. How could the cross be beautiful?
 III. Christ endured the cross for you.
    A. His death was sacrificial.
    B. The cross is beautiful to the eyes of faith.
 IV. The Christ of the cross calls you to bear your crosses.
    A. You bear crosses because of your confession.
    B. Crosses are beautiful to the eye of faith.

Sermon: The Cross of Suffering

1 Peter 2:21–25

Look at the cross that holds our attention this evening. It has a certain fascination—a beauty perhaps unequaled by any other form of the cross. Its arms are all of equal length, perfectly symmetrical. That is why it is called "the Greek Cross." Perfect symmetry was a mark of beauty to the Greeks, and they loved beauty even in instruments of torture such as the cross.

On Beautifying the Cross

It sounds strange, does it not, to speak of "beautifying" the cross? How can such a horrible instrument of death be made beautiful in any sense of the term? Why would anyone even try to do it?

Efforts at "beautifying" the cross are by no means confined to the way the Greeks fashioned this example, however. They continue right into our own day. So the questions are not merely asked of the Greeks; we must answer them ourselves.

How do we beautify the cross? It is subtle, but it happens very readily. It is difficult for us to think of a terrible instrument of punishment as an instrument of God's salvation. Somehow we feel compelled to make what God does more pleasing to our senses, more acceptable. So it is tempting to make it appear to be something less. Thus we tone it down and thereby keep God from appearing too earthy.

This can be done by emphasizing that "God so loved the world" that He gave His Son over to the cross. God's love always sounds nice and neat. Surely sacrificial acts done out of love do not hurt as much as things that we experience out of necessity. That *ought* to be true, anyway. So we make a Greek Cross on which God's love in part overcomes hurt and pain, thus minimizing the suffering of Christ. We don't say it like that, and we know it is mixed up with sin, so we can't take all the messiness out of it, but somehow it helps us to satisfy our urge to make the cross nicer than what it really was. So the joy of Christ's sacrifice makes it possible to retain the cross, just as the Greeks retained the form of the cross while beautifying it, without having to think too much about its pain and anguish.

This can, in fact, be pressed further by stressing that the cross is a divine act performed by God made man, who does indeed feel something of our human suffering while His divinity permits Him to rise above all that we go through. This easily transforms the cross into its Greek form by acknowledging His suffering and death while never really relating it to our own life, suffering, and death, because it all happens almost as a divine and heavenly act. How can God feel like us, even on a cross? A Greek Cross asks that kind of question.

A final step in this process happens when people barely stop at the cross long enough to tip their hat to it, hurrying on by to view the resurrection, which is much more pleasant to consider. It is not unusual to hear complaints about crucifixes in church because of a preference for the empty cross, since a dead Christ without the resurrection means nothing. But to rush to the resurrection without any real understanding of the crucifixion is to belittle the cross, beautifying it by rather subtly but very really ignoring it in favor of the resurrection. This is the ultimate Greek form of the cross.

Perhaps here we come close to the heart of why people want to make this instrument of our redemption beautiful. One discloses one's view of life and death by the way one views the cross. There are those who propose that life is essentially intended to be happy, reasonably successful, and largely carefree and sublime—at least in large measure. It is undeniable, of course, that terrible intrusions of suffering and pain and distress interrupt this flow toward happiness. But these are indeed intrusions and should be dealt with by hurrying through them, lightening them as best we can, and ignoring them if at all possible. It is a particular temptation of our time and culture to speak of and search for a life without pain in which perpetual pleasure and ever intensifying happiness, increasing success, and immediate solutions to problems are emphasized. We see monumental problems solved in 60 minutes of a television show; drugs deaden our pain; healthy diets and proper exercise programs promise happy and long lives; and lawyers guard our every sensitivity from someone who offends us or causes us distress. That is seeing life as a Greek Cross, a sort of minimal burden overshadowed by beauty that all but dismisses the pain. When life is viewed in this fashion, death is pushed into the background, and it is very difficult to comprehend fully the dimensions of Jesus' real cross. So why bother stopping to look at it too long in meditative contemplation?

Life as a Cross

Although the life just described is often spoken of as a sort of ideal of our time, few people experience it like that. Nor did Jesus. His cross had its beginning long before He hung on it. The shadow of Herod's sword lay across His manger cradle from birth. Little though we know of His life before His entrance on His public ministry, one can be sure that He shared the burdens we commonly carry. Could He have lived for 30 years without knowing the pain and suffering of people around Him as well as His own need to care for those in His own household and the concerns of a carpentry shop? Could He have been free of all temptation until that moment after His baptism when the Spirit led Him into the wilderness, or did He not know of the strife and division within His own country and religious community and of Israel's longing to be free of Roman rule? Surely He was conscious of social, political, psychological, physical, and religious concerns and cares as we are.

Jesus' life as well as His death (for they really must be joined in many ways) forms the backdrop for Peter's admonition to those addressed in the text. He wrote, "Slaves, submit yourselves to your masters with all respect, not only to those who are good and considerate, but also to those who are harsh. For it is commendable if a man bears up under the pain of unjust suffering because he is conscious of God." So our text is set within an admonition to servants. Earlier they have been told that they were ransomed from all that once bound them, made free by God's redeeming activity in Christ. Now these free people are urged to be servants of the highest caliber, giving themselves over to suffering as God's people if that becomes necessary. They are free to serve (although at first hearing they may have preferred to be free *from* service). They are free to suffer (although they may have preferred hearing that they were free *from* suffering).

Without the backdrop of Jesus' life and death, these would be strange admonitions. But Peter makes plain that this way is placed before them "because Christ suffered for you, leaving you an example, that you should follow in his steps." Nor is this the only place or the only group of people to whom he addresses words like this. "Therefore, since Christ suffered in his body, arm yourselves also with the same attitude," he urges all his readers (4:1). "Do not be surprised at the painful trial you are suffering, as though something strange were happening to you. But rejoice that you participate in the sufferings of Christ," he adds (vv, 12–13).

One would think Peter was a masochist, loving to suffer and be punished, if he were not making Christ his constant point of reference. But he makes plain that this suffering is not to be sought out nor to be endured for doing silly or wrong things. "But how is it to your credit if you receive a beating for doing wrong and endure it? But if you suffer for doing good and you endure it, this is commendable before God. To this you were called" (2:20–21). And there is that thought again that haunts the cross: "to this you have been called." How is suffering tied to godly living? Why does it seem necessary to have a cross if one is godly?

The Cross: Death to Old Life—Doorway to New

Suffering is tied to godliness because Christ's death is tied to a life that cuts across the flow of the world. And the world does not like that, nor does it tolerate it for long without assaulting it and crucifying it.

One can see that exemplified in Christ's life, His 33-year cross that is finally planted on Calvary. He was not crucified for the events of one day or for two or three inflammatory sayings. His crucifixion flowed out of a life that cut across the grain of the world's thinking and living. That is why, in order to offset the beautifying effect of the Greek Cross, it is very commonly found in a sequence of five, one cross for each of Jesus' wounds. Thus the horror and agony of the cross is set against its beauty, and reality is restored to it.

The cross in this way sets forth the beauty of one who "committed no sin, and no deceit was found in his mouth. When they hurled their insults at him, he did not retaliate; when he suffered, he made no threats. Instead, he entrusted himself to him who judges justly" (vv. 22–23). Yet with the five crosses we are also reminded of the awfulness of the cross where "he himself bore our sins in his body on the tree, so that we might die to sin and live for righteousness; by his wounds you have been healed" (v. 24).

So the cross calls you to two things. On the one hand, it calls you to know how deeply the very heart of God suffered for you. It tells of the five wounds of Jesus, the agony of dying by exposure with nails piercing hands and feet and thorns crushing down on His fevered brow while a gradual suffocation took its toll on His body weakened by the cruel blows of soldiers and the whipping administered under Pilate's order. But it tells more, for through the cross we have a window into the very heart of God, who stood by as though helpless. The One who could have stopped everything and relieved His Son stands by as though bound by our sins to permit this terrible torture. It is bad enough to suffer oneself, but when a Father must watch His Son suffer and stand by without doing anything about it, the torment is unbelievable. So the cross shows you the very heart of the Father, whose love sends His Son for you while it tells of the immense sacrifice the Son willingly made for you. Now the words willingly and joyfully can enter the picture not to make the cross more beautiful but to tell you how terrible it was. One who did not need to die gave Himself freely, willingly, even joyfully into death because through it "you [who] were like sheep going astray ... have returned to the Shepherd and Overseer of your souls" (v. 25). Here you can see with what intensity Peter speaks when he says, "By his wounds you have been healed." This is such a terrible day that the Spirit, who drew back the darkness on the first day of creation to reveal light, now draws it back to cover the earth again during the last hours before Jesus breathes His last.

The five Greek Crosses tell you of the suffering of God on your behalf—and on behalf of all humankind across the ages. It is a terrible cross. Yet it is at the same time the most beautiful of all crosses, for by it and through it God has called you and me back to Himself.

This is the second message of the Greek Cross. It tells you that you yourself were beautified through this cross. Your sins are taken away through this cross. All that makes the world in general and you in particular ugly is beautified in this marvelous moment. The door is opened to a new life.

This new life, of course, is not all that easy, for it is, in turn, a call to follow the Man of the cross—and therefore, like Simon of Cyrene, to carry His cross yourself. Although you are beautified through this gracious act of God, the dust settles all too quickly again both around you and within you. Your call to new life is not easily carried out—and it will be a life of suffering.

Part of that suffering is an inner awareness of how far short you fall in that new walk, in that calling to which "you were called" to follow Jesus. Thoughts, words, and deeds that are even shameful in your own eyes crop up and overwhelm you regularly. You suffer within yourself by knowing you are not even what you would like to be, much less what God calls you to be. And you suffer with Christ when you realize that this very shortfall in your life burdens Him on the cross. His suffering becomes yours in these moments.

Another part of that suffering comes from outside of you as your life carries the name of Christ written large over it. The world loves to see you stumble and fall, to be like it. If or when that happens, you suffer with Christ as the world scoffs at you. Christ's suffering is your suffering when these taunts and jeers are hurled at you and at Him. On the other hand, when you are indeed Christ-like, the world pulls and tugs at you to get you off your "pedestal," as the world may put it, so that you are just like it. And the wounds of Christ become your wounds as the world demands that you be like it is or it will crucify you.

So you wear the Greek Cross as a mark of following Christ—to show the awful price of redemption and your willingness to be wounded in His name but also to show the beauty of God's love and the glory of the new life that He makes possible.

Wear it proudly. It reminds us of the gateway to eternity.

Week of Lent 5

Cross Crosslet—Mission

Sermon Study

Text: Ephesians 2:14–18
Passion Reading: Luke 24:45–47

Introduction

"Money poured down a rat hole" was one layman's description of mission dollars. His pastor was shocked (we hope the laypeople were too!) because the statement was so unconventional. Mission ranks with the proverbial "apple pie and motherhood" as a safe topic about which to preach. There are few people who do not at least pay lip service to the task of spreading the Gospel. But if you intensify your mission efforts to an ethnic minority in your town, to convicts, to the chemically dependent, to homosexuals, in short, to all those who are different than we are, then mission can become a controversial and shocking topic. Variations of the "separate but equal" approach will be offered as convenient ways to protect our sinful prejudices and ease our guilt about evangelizing others: "Let them have their own church. They'd feel uncomfortable with us anyway." In this final midweek service we do not want merely to mouth the Great Commission; we want to proclaim a wonderful result of mission: Peace for hostile people who are made one in the cross of Christ.

The Cross Crosslet is appropriate for this week's theme. The four Latin crosses point to the four corners of the earth, symbolizing the command to "go into all the world and preach the good news to all creation" (Mark 16:15). The four crosses are united at the base, suggesting that all the different people of the world—including those close to home, the groups of your community—are made one in Christ. As Paul says in this week's text: "He [i.e., Christ] himself is our peace, who has made the two [Jew and Gentile] one and has destroyed the barrier, the dividing wall of hostility" (Eph. 2:14–15).

The Crosslet has been reserved for the last midweek Lenten service for a practical reason. "C & E (Christmas and Easter) Christians" and those who are completely unchurched will be coming to your services in the next weeks. Whether they have been invited to attend a confirmation or feel obligated to go to church on Easter, these prospects will present themselves to you to be evangelized. Some of the pillars of your congregation will resent those who seldom darken the threshold of your church. Some of the prospects, in turn, will resent the old, faithful members of the church. All in all, it offers a golden opportunity for mission, the mission that unites different and at times hostile people in the cross of Jesus Christ. His cross can break down the walls of hostility.

Background: The Wall of Hostility and Jewish Mission

Paul wasn't the kind of Christian who paid lip service to mission but kept his old prejudices. Even during his days as a young Pharisee under Gamaliel, he knew that the Old Testament had a missionary thrust. Isaiah had promised that the temple would attract the Gentiles:

> *In the last days the mountain of the Lord's*
> *temple will be established as chief among*
> *the mountains; it will be raised above the*
> *hills, and all nations will stream to it. Many*
> *peoples will come and say, 'Come, let us go*
> *up to the mountain of the Lord, to the house*
> *of God of Jacob. He will teach us his ways,*
> *so that we may walk in his paths.'*
> *(Is. 2:2–3)*

An amazing promise later in Isaiah shows the Lord uniting nations that had been at odds:

> *In that day there will be a highway from*
> *Egypt to Assyria. The Assyrians will go to*
> *Egypt and the Epyptians to Assyria. The*
> *Epyptians and Assyrians will worship to-*
> *gether. In that day Israel will be the third,*
> *along with Egypt and Assyria, a blessing on*
> *the earth. The Lord Almighty will bless them,*
> *saying, "Blessed be Egypt my people, Assyria*
> *my handiwork, and Israel my inheritance."*
> *(19:23–25)*

Other Old Testament passages on mission include Psalms 22, 65, and 86 and Jonah. Paul and the Pharisees knew that God wanted the Gentiles in His kingdom.

Yet the hostility between Jews and Gentiles in the first century dulled the mission thrust of the Old Testament. The Jews of the first century were not unconscious of mission. The synagogue worship service began with Eighteen Benedictions, one of which was a prayer for converts. A certain Rabbi Eleazar said "God scattered Israel among the nations for the sole end that proselytes should wax numerous among them." Jesus noted the Pharisees mission activity in Matthew 23:15: "You travel over land and sea to win a single convert." But these encouraging signs of mission activity were accompanied by strong indications of Jewish hostility for Gentiles. Jesus' ministry is filled with incidents reflecting the hatred of Jew and Gentile. A bitter statement from Simeon ben Yohai of the early second century shows that missions was not as sweet a topic as apple pie and motherhood: "Kill the best of the Gentiles; crush the head of the best of snakes." A shocking statement, to be sure, but it reflects the environment in which Paul and his contemporaries lived. Bringing Jews and Gentiles together was controversial business.

The Damascus road didn't make it any less controversial. The Lord told Ananias that Paul was "my chosen instrument to carry my name before the Gentiles and their kings and before the people of Israel" (Acts 9:15). When we refer to Paul as the great missionary to the Gentiles, we may forget that much of his labors were directed toward the people of Israel. When he moved into a new mission field, he began his efforts at the synagogue and continued there as long as possible. He followed that pattern at Ephesus, demonstrating that mission is not just telling somebody about Jesus but becoming with them a part of the new person, the body of Christ.

Context: The Work in Ephesus and the Letter to the Ephesians

Ephesus proved to be a long and productive stop on Paul's third missionary journey. He began his work in the synagogue with a nucleus of 12 believers who knew of Christ but not of the Holy Spirit. As Paul's work was blessed, opposition to him became stronger, and he was forced to move his daily discussions from the synagogue to the lecture hall of Tyrannus. His three years of labor were productive; Luke tells us that "all the Jews and Greeks who lived in the province of Asia heard the word of the Lord" (Acts 19:10). When a silversmith named Demetrius saw that the Christian mission was cutting into his sales of idols, he instigated a riot that forced Paul to leave Ephesus. Some time later he met with the Ephesian elders at Miletus and reminded them that "I have declared to both Jews and Greeks that they must turn to God in repentance and have faith in our Lord Jesus" (Acts 20:21). Paul's mission was to unite Jew and Gentile in the one body of Christ.

That glorious mission drew enemy fire when Paul arrived in Jerusalem. He was arrested on the charge of defiling the temple because he allegedly brought a Gentile into the holy area.

Some Jews from the province of Asia saw Paul at the temple. They stirred up the whole crowd and seized him, shouting, "Men of Israel, help us! This is the man who teaches all men everywhere against our people and our law and this place. And besides, he has brought Greeks into the temple area and defiled this holy place.... The whole city was aroused, and the people came running from all directions. (Acts 21:27–30)

Such animosity towards Gentiles at the temple, the place God intended as a "house of prayer for all nations" (Is. 56:7)! The rabbis' lip service to mission was a veneer over sin working hostility through the Law.

During his imprisonment for allegedly defiling the temple, Paul wrote to the Ephesians to celebrate the union of Jew and Gentile in Christ. Some scholars, noting the lack of personal references in the letter, suggest that it was to a general audience. Chapter 1 contains the traditional salutation and praise for God's redemptive plan. Chapter 2 speaks directly to the incorporation of the Gentiles. "You," he writes, "were dead in your transgressions and sins" (2:1), but "God, who is rich in mercy, made us alive with Christ even when we were dead in transgressions—it is by grace you have been saved" (2:5). Jew and Gentile are one. Those evangelized in all corners of the world find themselves bound together at the cross.

Text: Ephesians 2:14–18

> *For he himself is our peace, who has made*
> *the two one and has destroyed the barrier,*
> *the dividing wall of hostility, by abolishing*
> *in his flesh the law with its commandments*
> *and regulations. His purpose was to create*
> *in himself one new man out of the two, thus*
> *making peace, and in this one body to rec-*
> *oncile both them to God through the cross,*
> *by which he put to death their hostility. He*
> *came and preached peace to you who were*
> *far away and peace to those who were near.*
> *For through him we both have access to the*
> *Father by one Spirit.*

Verse 14: "He himself is our peace." This is the first of four times the word "peace" occurs in the sermon text (vv. 14, 15, 17). The word "hostility" occurs twice (vv. 14, 16). There is more to this text than a recital of the Great Commission. Rather, we see what God does through mission: He makes peace for hostile people. That peace is not a byproduct of proclaiming Christ; it is Christ himself. He himself is peace as He incorporates disparate people into His body, the church. He is the Prince of Peace, who will lead wolf and lamb, leopard and goat in the messianic age (Is. 9:6; 11:6).

Verses 14b–15a: "Who has made the two one and has destroyed the barrier, the dividing wall of hostility, by abolishing in his flesh the law with its commandments and regulations." When Paul wrote of "the barrier, the dividing wall of hostility," he may have had a mental picture of the wall that separated the court of the Gentiles from the temple proper. Death was promised to any Gentile who passed that wall. The hostility of the peoples separated by that wall focused on the Jewish law.

> *The Law of the Jews, which consisted in in-*
> *numerable regulations, definite commands,*
> *and prohibitions, repelled the Gentiles and*
> *awakened in them a certain animosity*
> *against the Jews when the latter tried to play*
> *the schoolmasters of the heathen. That is a*
> *common experience. The Law with its mo-*
> *notonous, insistent repetitions, "thou shalt,"*
> *and "thou shall not," neither attracts the*

natural man nor wins his love; it rather re-
pels him. (George Stoeckhardt, Commentary
on St. Paul's Letter to the Ephesians, trans.
Martin S. Sommer [St. Louis: Concordia Pub-
lishing House, 1952], p. 147)

Christ came to fulfill the Law (Matt. 5:17; Rom. 10:4) and becomes the criterion for entrance into the people of God. "In his flesh," that is, in His body (cf. Rom. 1:3), He ended the supremacy of the Law with its unremitting demands.

Verses 15b–16: "His purpose was to create in himself one new man out of the two, thus making peace, and in this one body to reconcile both of them to God through the cross, by which he put to death their hostility." On this new man Thomas Abbott cites Chrysostom: "Not ... that He has brought us to that nobility of theirs, but both us and them to a greater; as if one should melt down a statue of silver and one of lead, and the two should come out gold" (A Critical and Exegetical Commentary on the Epistles to the Ephesians, p. 61). This union takes place in the body of Christ, the church, just as the Crosslet has four Latin crosses united at the base. The new peace between Jew and Gentile is the result of the peace that all mankind now has with God, a reconciliation earned at the cross (cf. Col. 1:20).

Verse 17: "He came and preached peace to you who were far away and peace to those who were near." Paul had used this "far" and "near" imagery in verse 13 to refer to Gentiles and Jews. This preaching refers to the early church's fulfillment of the Great Commission (cf. Luke 24:45–47; Rom. 10:16), an activity still carried on by the faithful today. Both Jew and Gentile were the target audience of the proclamation of peace. So today, faithful Christians will benefit from the reminder that they are part of the picture. They as much as any people benefit from the work of Christ. Hence their zeal for mission comes from the Gospel, not from the Law. "Witness is not a burden laid upon the Church. It is not a part of the law. It is gospel, gift, promise. We misinterpret the whole thrust of the New Testament when we convert this into a law, a burden laid upon the consciences of Christians" (Lesslie Newbigin, Sign of the Kingdom [Grand Rapids, Mich.: Eerdmans, 1981], p. 37).

Verse 18: "For through him we both have access to the Father by one Spirit." The theme of unity is climaxed by this Trinitarian verse. Our unity is a work of the entire godhead.

Sermon Starters

Central thought: The proclamation of Christ in mission work brings peace to hostile peoples.

Outline 1: **"And Give You Peace"**
I. The Cross Crosslet: Mission to the four corners of the world
II. Many hostile people

A. Current hostilities
B. The hostility between Jew and Gentile in the first century
C. Do you feel hostility?
   1. Against some mission fields?
   2. Against some people in town who need to be evangelized?

III. Christ our peace
A. Crosslet: Four crosses are united at the base.
B. Christ destroyed hostility
   1. between Jew and Gentile;
   2. between hostile peoples today;
   3. between you and evangelism prospects who are "different than we are."
C. Most important, Christ is our peace with God!

IV. Crosslet
A. Mission proclamation to four corners, to hostile peoples
B. Peace together in Christ

V. Conclusion: As you leave church to go on His mission, He gives you peace.

Outline 2: Don't Divide, Multiply!

I. The Cross Crosslet: Mission to the four corners of the world
II. Mission to hostile peoples
A. Many Berlin walls
B. Wall in temple separating Jew and Gentile
C. Sometimes even hostility for mission and evangelism prospects
III. Christ destroyed the dividing wall.
A. Ended the hostility between Jew and Gentile
B. Makes two into one
C. Crosslet: United at the base; no division
IV. Don't divide—multiply!
A. Luke 24:45–47
B. Early church went to the four corners of the world
C. Starting from the cross, we too will multiply!

Outline 3: Centrifugal and Centripetal Mission

I. Strange title
A. Explanation of centrifugal and centripetal
B. The way of mission
   1. Impelled outward from the cross
   2. to bring people to the cross.
C. Symbolized by the Cross Crosslet
II. Centrifugal mission into all the world
A. Luke 24:45–47
B. Early Church
C. Today
III. Centripetal peace: Christ brings hostile people together.
A. Christ brings us together.

1. The cross is the center of His ministry.
    2. He overcame the hostility that drives people from one another.
  B. Christian mission unites different peoples at the cross.
    1. Jew and Gentile
    2. Different peoples today
IV. Crosslet: Centrifugal and centripetal mission

Sermon: The Missions Crosslet

Ephesians 2:14–18

Dreams have been powerful forces on occasion in the course of history. Some dreams have come from beyond the conscious power of the dreamer as when he or she is asleep. We remember the strength Jacob drew from his dream of angels ascending and descending the ladder into heaven. We remember also Joseph's dream that infuriated his brothers and got him a free trip to Egypt and then the dream of the Pharaoh as a result of which Joseph rose to second in command in Egypt, saving the land from the ravages of famine and getting his family into Egypt. Or we remember Peter's dream in which unclean food was placed before him and God commanded him to eat it, thus opening the door to the earliest proclamation of the Gospel to the Gentiles.

Other dreams have been born of conscious reflection on the part of the dreamer. Martin Luther King's famous speech in front of the Lincoln Memorial in Washington, D. C., focused on the phrase, "I have a dream." Robert Kennedy popularized the phrase, "You see things as they are and ask why. But I dream things that never were and ask why not." That phrase describes quite well the way some people look around themselves, envisioning how a new set of circumstances could change things and then setting themselves to the task of reshaping the world. They, too, are "dreamers," and the world is moved by such people.

The Dream

Such a dream once swept over a man with such force that it changed the course of Christian history—and thereby began to reshape the history of the entire world. Whether it involved conscious reflection in dreamlike images or whether it came on him in a sleep or trance is hard to tell. When one dreams, it is hard to know for sure the source of the dream.

It was as though the vague outline of a beckoning finger lured him irresistibly into a dark and fearful passageway. Although alone, he felt the awesome presence of whoever was attached to this beckoning finger as he edged along the terrifying way.

Gradually he felt less and less fear even though the eery darkness still surrounded him. Finally, suddenly, he felt an immense calm surrounding him and within him. The path was now clearly well trodden. Suddenly he came to a small anteroom within which a peace of heretofore unimagined magnitude came over him. All the burdens and cares that had ever beset him were lifted.

Now the vague shape of the beckoning finger began to take on visible form. The figure now revealed told the dreamer that the peace of this place was nothing less than the peace of God, for he had been descending deeper and deeper into the heart of God on this journey. Here one need never again want and all tears would be wiped away.

His heart jumped with joy, for this had been his goal in life. Was he now dead? Whatever the case, he was prepared to remain for a long, long stay. He hoped it would be an eternal one.

But with a start he heard the guide tell him that, having now experienced this, he must decide whether to pass through the door beyond the anteroom or to return to life as he had known it before this journey. The anteroom was no permanent place, he was told. One must return or go forward.

Surely there was no desire to return, but there was considerable fear in going forward. What more could there possibly be? Why could he not simply remain here? He could not now live with less, and he could not imagine more. It was a fearful thing, but he tried the door.

It was locked!

The guide, now become the doorkeeper, placed a key into the lock, turned it and opened the door for the dreamer to pass through. The light was blinding at first, and he saw nothing. One thing only did he know in that first moment—the peace he had experienced before continued and, if possible, was even enriched. So he had lost nothing. But what had he gained? For the first time on the journey he heard voices other than that of his guide.

As he became accustomed to the light, he saw people of every sort gathered around. Some may well have been friends under earlier circumstances, but many were people with whom he knew full well he would never have associated. But there they were—people of every kind and sort surrounding him. He had never seen such a gathering.

"In the anteroom," his guide said, "you discovered how deeply God's love touches you with peace. But you cannot keep that peace in solitude. God's love encompasses and surrounds people of every sort. One can sense its magnitude alone, but its total fullness cannot be known save when in the company of all those held in His heart.

"That is why you could not stay in the anteroom. You either had to return or to discover those who share this peace with you here in the heart of God. Nor can you remain here in this peace if you choose to break it. In other words, should you even so much as wish one of these, God's loved ones, out of His heart, you shall be returned immediately to that place from which you came."

He looked around, realizing what sort of company he would have to keep from now on if he wished to remain.

And he awakened with a start.

Putting the Dream into Words

Now the dreamer wondered what the dream might mean. He reviewed it in orderly fashion as he now consciously reflected on it.

What was disturbing was that the dream went contrary to everything he had believed in earlier life. He had grown up among people calling themselves "the chosen of God" and "the elect." Although outsiders could be incorporated into their midst (and were even sought by some), by and large it was considered important to remain aloof from people who were different lest they become contaminated by "outside influences." Their separateness from others was precisely to keep themselves clean of everything that might separate them from God so that they might remain close to God. So the separateness had been good—a matter of conscience and necessary for godliness, in fact.

But the beckoning finger had led him down a dark and forbidding passageway. He shuddered as he thought of it again, but somehow it seemed so much a part of him that it had not been strange even though it was forbidding. It suddenly occurred to him that it was nothing other than the passageway through his own inner being, through his own heart. It was the dark cavern that he himself had carefully dug out to conceal things he wanted to hide from others—things that frightened even himself when he had to confront them. It had the jagged edges of his own hasty burial of things about which he was ashamed and over which he felt much remorse. It smelled of the mildew of almost forgotten places in his life.

The way had changed as they went on, and he wondered if perhaps in his dream the passageway into and through the heart of God had been joined to his own heart's passageway. That accounted for the peace that came on him. He had moved from his own heart into the heart of God. Where his old ways had ended and had been joined to a new way, it throbbed with a different spirit. There he had sensed a mending of his spirit, a sense of peace pervading his whole being.

This way was well trodden because it had been joined to many hearts before his. It was certain, at any rate, that he felt truly at home on this new path. The calm came from the awareness, particularly as that strange, beckoning finger began to take on a shape, that God Himself was present with him. That was his peace and his joy.

But at just that moment he had been told that he must pass through the door or return. He had reached for the door, but it could only be opened with the key. Now he remembered that the key had been shaped like a cross. In fact, that was precisely what it was—a cross.

The cross had opened the door to the blinding light and to all those other people. They, too, had come on this path when it had been joined to their hearts. They, too, had stood in that antechamber and watched the cross unlock the door to this light and this peace—and to each other. Here, in the presence of the Father, Son, and Holy Spirit, those who were called by His name and had been baptized into that name now gloried in the company of God and each other. People of every sort were caught up into His heart, many of whom had been outsiders before joining this company encompassed by God's love. In his previous life it would have appeared so wrong, but here in the heart of God it was all so very, very right. Their differences were covered by the blazing glory of God permeating them all so that none were different even while all were different.

The dreamer struggled to find words to describe what that vision meant. Finally he wrote:

> For he himself is our peace, who has made
> the two one and has destroyed the barrier,
> the dividing wall of hostility, by abolishing
> in his flesh the law with its commandments
> and regulations. His purpose was to create
> in himself one new man out of the two, thus
> making peace, and in this one body to rec-
> oncile both of them to God through the
> cross, by which he put to death their hostil-
> ity. He came and preached peace to you who
> were far away and peace to those who were
> near. For through him we both have access
> to the Father by one Spirit.

That is our text for this evening.

The Message of the Crosslet

It is doubtful, of course, that Paul ever had such a dream. It was made up to illustrate the text. But it is a dream that flows out of the text even though it did not originally create the text. It is a way of helping you see the inside of the text.

And it is a way of helping you see the message of the Crosslet holding our attention on this last Wednesday evening before Holy Week. The Crosslet is made up of four Latin crosses pointing to the four corners of the world. It symbolizes the command to "go into all the world and preach the good news to all creation" (Mark 16:15). The four crosses are united at the base, suggesting that all the different people of the world (including your church or community) are made one in Christ. As Paul writes, "[Christ] himself is our peace, who has made the two [Jew and Gentile—and all others at odds with or separated from one another] one and has destroyed the barrier, the dividing wall of hostility" (Eph. 2:14).

You are the one who stands squarely in the center of this cross—or in reality, this series of crosses. The four crosses point to the four corners of the earth, your community, or your life. You yourself have come to this center place through the cross that points outward.

But you are not alone. Many others are here with you. And the cross beckons many others to come its way also. That means that this evening's Crosslet, enlightened by Paul's words in the text, unfolded in dreamlike fashion, has a two-fold message and mission for you.

The first message and mission urges you to foster peace in the place where the cross is planted. It asks where there may be discord in your life and how you might take a new measure of that discord by the peace planted in you. How does this peace given to you in the forgiveness made available to you on the cross work its way out into your family, your neighbors, your acquaintances, your church, your community, and your world? The word "peace" occurs four times within the short span of this text while "hostility" appears twice. The tension between the two is clear, and it calls us to the task of making peace precisely where hostility has such a strong presence among us.

So the first message urges you toward the mission of making peace in the midst of hostility. You are invited into the heart of God to find what life there is like—and to live it that way on earth.

The second message and mission is equally as urgent. It has to do with those who still do not know the peace of God so prominent in the dream born of our text.

The Crosslet points us in all directions—to the end of the earth, to our community, or to our acquaintances. It reaches into the corners of where we live and work. It urges us to remember brothers and sisters in the far parts of the world and in our own circles of acquaintances who still have not found this peace of God and to tell them about it, show it to them by the way you live, and invite them to join you there, deep in the heart of God.

This text and the Crosslet are appropriate for this last Wednesday before we enter on the week called holy, when we will remember again the suffering, death, and resurrection of our Lord. It is a good time—dare we say, "the *right* time"?—for you to take the message of the Crosslet and this text seriously, turning it into the mission of speaking the word of invitation to those around you. These are days for holding the cross high before your family and friends and neighbors. These are days for reconciliation with those in whom you have felt some of the hostility spoken of in the text, inviting them, rather, to know the peace of him "who has made the two one, and has destroyed the barrier, the dividing wall of hostility."

Turn the dream into the reality of your life. God did, and now He calls you to do it.

Maundy Thursday

Celtic Cross—Redemption

Sermon Study

Text: *Colossians 1:19–23*

Introduction

"If the ox could paint a picture, his god would look like an ox." These words of Xenophanes, a fifth-century B.C. critic of Greek religion, were not aimed at oxen but at people and their gods. It's logical, Xenophanes thought, for people to think of their gods in human form. Since certain knowledge of the divine is impossible, we can only have unsure opinions. Who can know for sure what God is really like?

Paul answers, "God was pleased to have all his fullness dwell in him [Christ]" (Col. 1:19). This opening sentence of the Maundy Thursday sermon text replaces Xenophanes' rubric (people project their own image on the divine) with the rubric of incarnation. To know the divine, its mystery, its wisdom, and its order, look at Christ. He is the Lord of eternity, who came to the cross to accomplish an eternal redemption.

The Celtic Cross brings the eternal into focus at the cross. Also called the Wheel Cross, the Cross of Iona, or the Irish Cross, its circle signifies eternity. The cross, of course, is a temporal instrument, something with which only the human and incarnate must contend. That we find eternity's Lord securing an eternal redemption at the cross is the theme of our Maundy Thursday worship. Xenophanes would scoff, but not your hearers. They are like the Colossians to whom Paul writes: "We have heard of your faith in Christ Jesus and of the love you have for all the saints" (Col. 1:4).

Maundy Thursday Background: Eternity's Lord Shows Himself to Be an Earthly Redeemer

Although Lord of eternity, supreme over "things in heaven and on earth, visible and invisible, whether thrones or powers or rulers or authorities" (v. 16), Christ became incarnate ("in Christ all the fullness of the Deity lives in bodily form," 2:9) and in that physical body reconciled all things to God with a redemption that lasts forever. The motion of the eternal coming down to the earthly was demonstrated by the Lord on the first Maundy Thursday.

Just before eating the Passover feast, Jesus washed the feet of the disciples. Washing dirty feet is certainly earthly business (compare the study in the Saltire Cross, the week of Lent 1, when the foot-washing episode demonstrated the Savior's humility). Peter thought it most inappropriate: "You shall never wash my feet" (John 13:8). But Jesus approached it as the eternal

Lord. He "knew that the Father had put all things under his power, and that he had come from God and was returning to God" (v. 3). Knowing His supreme power, He got down to His earthly task with these words: "You call me 'Teacher' and 'Lord,' and rightly so, for that is what I am. Now that I, your Lord and Teacher, have washed your feet, you also should wash one another's feet. I have set you an example" (vv. 13–15).

Jesus did more on Maundy Thursday than give us an example. In the institution of His supper, the eternal Lord recognizes that we, His creatures, are bound by earthly limitations, and so He came (and comes) to us in elements that we know and can receive. Bread and wine are common elements. There certainly is nothing exotic about bread, and the increase in wine consumption by Americans is evidence that we no longer regard wine as a rich man's drink. Yet the eternal Lord comes to His finite children in these elements: "This is my body." "This is my blood." Xenophanes and the Colossian heretics, as we shall soon see, would have found this all a bit too pedestrian. They wanted their spirits to ascend to eternal realms without eternity's Lord coming down to live with them as a man.

Only because He did that could the Colossian faithful and the faithful today participate in an eternal redemption. As the motion of Maundy Thursday spirals downward from the eternal to the earthly, so by the common elements of bread and wine God lifts His baptized people (and isn't water common, too?) to participation in His eternal redemption. He takes us beyond the limitations of sense, reason, and time and gives us a foretaste of the heavenly banquet, uniting us with all the saints on earth and in heaven.

> *And he said to them, "I have eagerly desired*
> *to eat this Passover with you before I suffer.*
> *For I tell you, I will not eat it again until it*
> *finds fulfillment in the kingdom of God."*
> *After taking the cup, he gave thanks and*
> *said, "Take this and divide it among you.*
> *For I tell you I will not drink again of the*
> *fruit of the vine until the kingdom of God*
> *comes" (Luke 22:15–18).*

Context: Gazing into Eternity, Not Seeing the Cross

His actions on Maundy Thursday stand in marked contrast to what the Colossian heretics were promoting. Epaphras, the founder of this congregation in the Lycus Valley of Asia Minor (Col. 1:7), came to Paul in Rome for help in combating the heresy that had come of his parishioners—the idea of gazing at things eternal without seeing the cross. Paul was imprisoned at Rome, and it turned out that the two had plenty of time to talk. Epaphras was imprisoned with him (Philemon 23).

No doubt he told Paul the symptoms of the heresy. Cosmic confusion was one of its marks. The people were fascinated by the eternal, its creatures, its wisdom, and its implications for the present. One or more of the proponents claimed to be a heaven gazer. Paul later wrote, "Do not let anyone who delights in false humility and the worship of angels disqualify you for the prize. Such a person goes into great detail about what he has seen" (Col. 2:18). Sharing their vision of the eternal—actually, projecting themselves on the eternal—the heretics were most persuasive. They used "fine-sounding arguments" (v. 4) and "philosophy" (v. 8). They translated their lofty visions into practical rules for daily living: "Do not handle! Do not taste! Do not touch!" (v. 21). How many times haven't you been told, "Pastor, tell us what we should do?" It was all most appealing to the Colossians, and faithful Epaphras sought apostolic help to combat it.

Paul's answer was not to reject the eternal but to sort out the confusion. In terms of the image for this Maundy Thursday, Paul looks to eternity, the circle, but he does so by looking through the cross of the incarnate Lord. After the standard epistolary greeting and thanksgiving, he asks "God to fill you with the knowledge of his will through all spiritual wisdom and understanding" (1:9) so that they might "live a life worthy of the Lord and may please him in every way: ... growing in the knowledge of God" (v. 10). To do this the focus of all must be on Christ, eternity's Lord.

> *He is the image of the invisible God, the*
> *firstborn over all creation. For by him all*
> *things were created: things in heaven and on*
> *earth, visible and invisible, whether thrones*
> *or powers or rulers or authorities; all things*
> *were created by him and for him. He is be-*
> *fore all things, and in him all things hold*
> *together. And he is the head of the body, the*
> *church; he is the beginning and the firstborn*
> *from among the dead, so that in everything*
> *he might have the supremacy. (vv. 15–18)*

Looking at the eternal God is done only by looking at Christ. Otherwise there is confusion. The Colossian letter is Paul's commentary on his earlier words to the Romans: "Neither angels nor demons, neither the present nor the future, nor any powers ... will be able to separate us from the love of God that is in Christ Jesus our Lord" (Rom. 8:38–39).

Text: Colossians 1:19–23

> *God was pleased to have all his fullness*
> *dwell in him, and through him to reconcile*
> *to himself all things, whether things on earth*
> *or things in heaven, by making peace*
> *through his blood, shed on the cross. Once*
> *you were alienated from God and were ene-*
> *mies in your minds because of your evil be-*
> *havior. But now he has reconciled you by*
> *Christ's physical body through death to pres-*
> *ent you holy in his sight, without blemish*
> *and free from accusation—if you continue*

*in your faith, established and firm, not
moved from the hope held out in the gospel.
This is the gospel that you heard and that
has been proclaimed to every creature under
heaven, and of which I, Paul, have become a
servant.*

Verse 19: There has been discussion whether the subject is the personified "fullness" or "God." The NIV resolves it with this translation: "God was pleased to have all his fullness dwell in him." (Cf. 2:9: "In Christ all the fullness of the Deity lives in bodily form.") Fullness, *plērōma,* has been explained as proleptic; Paul is using a key term of the heretics. Just as much in the background is Old Testament usage. Ps. 68:16: "Why gaze in envy, O rugged mountains, at the mountain where God chooses to reign." 1 Kings 8:27: "Will God really dwell on earth? The heavens, even the highest heaven, cannot contain you. How much less this temple I have built!" Christ now replaces the temple as the place of God's dwelling on earth. The eternal Lord is found in bodily form.

Verse 20a: "and through him to reconcile to himself all things, whether things on earth or things in heaven." The stress is on "all things," including the supernatural powers that the heretics esteemed so highly. (Cf. 2:15: "And having disarmed the powers and authorities, he made a public spectacle of them, triumphing over them by the cross"; Rom. 8:38–39.) "Through him" is through Christ (cf. 1 Peter 1:21), and "himself" is God. Note that faith is not a condition of reconciliation. God through Christ has reconciled all things, whether we believe it or not.

Verse 20b: "by making peace through his blood, shed on the cross." The eternal Lord accomplishes redemption on a lowly cross. "Blood" is commonly used in reference to Christ's death because blood was equated with life (Lev. 17:11: "The life of a creature is in the blood.") Hence after the world's first murder, God says, "Your brother's blood cries out to me from the ground" (Gen. 4:10). Here as elsewhere the New Testament speaks of redemption by Christ's blood. "In him we have redemption through his blood" (Eph. 1:7; cf. also Acts 20:28; 1 Peter 1:19; Rev. 1:5; 5:9; 14:1–5; et al.). Blood has atoning power. On Maundy Thursday Christ offers this blood to His people: " 'This cup is the new covenant in my blood; do this, whenever you drink it, in remembrance of me.' For whenever you eat this bread and drink this cup, you proclaim the Lord's death until he comes" (1 Cor. 11:25–26). On the new covenant of Christ's blood see Jeremiah 31:31–34 and especially Hebrews 9:11–28.

Verse 21: "Once you were alienated from God and were enemies in your minds because of your evil behavior." The plural "you" is emphatic and brings Christ's work of reconciliation home to the readers. Their alienation from God had been complete, even their minds being set against God (cf. Rom. 1:28–32). As in Romans, their opposition to God revealed itself in evil deeds. Remember that those deeds were often done under the aegis of religion.

Verse 22: "But now he has reconciled you by Christ's physical body through death to present you holy in his sight, without blemish and free from accusation." On the first part of the verse, see notes on verse 20. The purpose of God's reconciliation is to have before Him a perfect people. The language here is similar to Ephesians 5:25–27: "Christ loved the church and gave himself up for her to make her holy, cleansing her by the washing with water through the word, and to present her to himself as a radiant church, without stain or wrinkle or any other blemish, but holy and blameless." "Free from accusation." Can we ever preach enough that Christ's work of redemption removes accusation? For a graphic description, read Zechariah 3. See also Romans 8:1. Friends and family may persist in accusing us for past sins, but God will not since His Son's work presents us as a holy people in His sight.

Verse 23a: "if you continue in your faith, established and firm, not moved from the hope held out in the gospel." This is a warning against the idea of "once in grace, always in grace." The imagery in this verse is that of a building. In Matthew 7:25 it is used of the person whose house (faith) is built on the rock (Jesus' Word). See also Ephesians 2:20. "Hope" is synonymous here with faith.

Verse 23b: "This is the gospel that you heard and that has been proclaimed to every creature under heaven, and of which I, Paul, have become a servant." Unlike the Colossian heretics, whose teachings were not for all, Paul's Gospel is proclaimed everywhere. (Cf 1:6: "all over the world.") The message of the eternal Lord's reconciliation of sinful humanity at the cross means we worship at a cross of universal redemption.

Sermon Starters

Central thought: At the cross, eternity's Lord secured our eternal redemption.

Outline 1:   **Bread, Wine, and the Celtic Cross**
I. Introduction: Maundy Thursday
  A. Our Lord institutes His supper.
  B. He selects common elements: bread and wine.
II. The eternal Lord comes to us.
  A. The Colossian heretics did not want a physical Lord.
  B. Paul's answer: God reconciled you through Christ's physical body at the cross.
III. The Celtic Cross
  A. The cross symbolizes physical reconciliation.
  B. The circle symbolizes its eternal value.
IV. Take bread and wine, take the Celtic Cross into your life.
  A. Don't minimize these common elements by which eternity's Lord comes to you.
  B. "Continue in your faith, established and firm."
V. Conclusion

A. We now celebrate His supper.

B. Eternity's Lord comes to us.

Outline 2: **A Picture of God**

 I. Introduction

A. Xenophanes: "If the ox could paint a picture, his god would look like an ox."

B. How do you picture God?

 II. Picture Him as a man.

A. "God was pleased to have all his fullness dwell in him."

B. The Redeemer is true man.

C. The Redeemer comes to us in Word and sacrament.

 III. Contrast: The god of imagination

A. People look for redemption apart from Word and sacrament, a god of their own imagination.

B. They follow the Colossian heretics, who imagined God without seeing the man of the cross.

 IV. Picture Him God and Man at the cross.

A. The cross in the Celtic Cross reminds us of the physical in our redemption.

B. The circle tells us that eternity's Lord secures an eternal redemption at the cross.

 V. Carry this picture with you.

Outline 3: **Theological Telescopes—The Celtic Cross**

 I. The problem

A. Then: The Colossians were so busy peering into eternity that they lost touch with the reality of the cross.

B. Today: People philosophize about God and forget the cross.

C. Theological telescopes

 II. The solution

A. Trade in those theological telescopes for the Celtic Cross.

B. The cross is reality.

1. The place of your redemption

2. "He has reconciled you by Christ's physical body through death."

3. The cross of the Celtic Cross symbolizes the reality of redemption.

C. The cross is where you see eternity.

1. "God was pleased to have all his fullness dwell in him."

2. The circle of the Celtic cross symbolizes your eternal redemption.

 III. The assignment

A. Do real theology in your life.

B. See the eternal at the cross of Christ.

Sermon: The Celtic Cross

Colossians 1:19–23

When you focus your attention on the cross that stands before us this evening, the Celtic Cross, you find symbolized the central truth to which the Christian faith attests: Salvation depends on God's taking up the form of our world and the burden of our world if we are to have any hope at all.

You all recognize, without doubt, the cross that stands out so prominently. It is an instrument of this earth, the cruel throne on which we humans seated the Lord of glory. The circle superimposed on the cross brings the eternal into focus, for the shape without beginning and without end is the sign of God. In this combination we find eternity's Lord securing an eternal redemption for us humans through an instrument of this earth, the cross.

Eternity Viewed Through Earthly Things

The Celtic Cross helps us gain an important understanding: God, who cannot be seen with human eyes, comes to His children on earth through earthly forms. To be even more specific, God comes to his children through Christ, in whom "God was pleased to have all his fullness dwell," and who most fully revealed God's will among us and toward us through His cross.

The very idea of God coming to earth through earthly forms was scandalous to the Greeks, and there were those in the Colossian congregation who had been affected by this notion also. They would go so far as to say that the only way we can talk about God is through human images. But they would never have gone so far as to say that God comes to humans through earthly forms.

The question of how to talk about God is a question of the ages. The Greek scandal has been a scandal to many others since then, for it is true that we can never see God. How, then, can you we talk accurately about something or someone whom we have never seen? Many people simply pass off all "God-talk" as philosophical or theoretical, saying that one can never say anything with any certainty about God.

Of course, it is true that God remains wrapped in mystery in many ways, but it is vital for the Christian to insist that God has made Himself known through the earthly person of Jesus of Nazareth. The Celtic Cross is one of many ways by which Christians try to signify this truth openly and boldly. On the cross the divine action was carried out in and through the bodily form of Jesus Christ. God's love became flesh-borne in the blood shed on the cross.

This truth that God comes among His children through earthly action and form is not confined to the New Testament, of course. On this very evening, for example, we remember the institution of the Lord's Supper, which was initiated at the Passover meal before Christ's crucifixion. The Passover meal commemorated that one dominant event to which Israel always turned when it wanted to talk about God. When God made Himself known in that great act of parting the waters so that His people could pass over on dry land, causing the waters to return over the pursuing army of Pharaoh, Israel was convinced that God's action in and through earthly events was the sign of His presence. That was the mark by which He was to be identified: "I am the Lord your God, who brought you out of Egypt, out of the land of slavery. You shall have no other gods before me" (Ex. 20:2–3).

From that time Israel always looked for the hand of God to be revealed within the realm of human history, on the plain of earthly action. Its whole history, including its captivity, exile, and return, were seen in this frame of reference: God, who cannot be seen through human eyes, comes to His children on earth through earthly actions and in earthly forms.

When it was proclaimed that Christ was the ultimate expression of this revelation of God through human form, that was not necessarily a jarring note within the framework of Israel's understanding. That it should be this particular man, Jesus of Nazareth, through whom God was revealing Himself was scandalous to many. But God had always made Himself known in the earthly dimension, and nothing made it impossible to think of Him as coming among them in and through a prophetic figure. It was not so much that God could not be present in one way or another through figures visible to the human eye that made His contemporaries reject Jesus. It was rather what seemed to be a presumptuous claim on Jesus' part that this unique manifestation was present in and through this one who seemed to have no credentials for the claim. Over and over they asked Him for "a sign."

The only "sign" he ever offered was, as he termed it, "the sign of Jonah," three days and nights swallowed up in the land of death. This, above all, was the scandal of Jesus Christ, that He claimed to be the presence of God among them and claimed as His sole power the power to serve those around Him. On this very night His own disciples were scandalized when Jesus, washing their feet, told them, "You call me 'Teacher' and 'Lord,' and rightly so, for that is what I am. Now that I, your Lord and Teacher, have washed your feet, you also should wash one another's feet" (John 13:13–14). This service, a continuation of a lifetime given to service and one that would climax on the next day with His humble suffering and death, was the way He "proved" that He was the Lord of the heavens on earth in the visible form of Jesus.

There was the scandal for everybody to think about.

It is the scandal put forth boldly in the Celtic Cross, signifying that the eternal God submitted to human needs on the very earthly cross through the very human Jesus of Nazareth. It scandalized many of the Jews of His time; it scandalized the Romans who outlawed the Christians for such claims; it scandalized some in the Colossian congregation, giving rise to Paul's letter; and it scandalizes people to this day.

But you and I live by the confession of St. Paul in our text: "For God was pleased to have all his fullness dwell in him, and through him to reconcile to himself all things, whether things on earth or things in heaven, by making peace through his blood, shed on the cross." The earthly blood of the divine Crucified One changes everything.

Earthly Things Viewed Through the Divine Eye

Surely everything needed to be changed. We catch a glimpse of what the earthly things look like from the eternal perspective in the text before us. "Once you were alienated from God and were enemies in your minds because of your evil behavior." With these words the divine eye tells us what it sees. And what I see is a long way from what the divine intention was in the original creation.

Those who were meant to be servants became those who struggled for mastery, and what was meant to be creature became idol. Those who were meant to be friends of God were now hostile, and what was meant for divine pleasure was now estranged. The Tower of Babel serves to this day as the great monument to human effort in every age—a monstrous attempt to achieve greatness and an eternal name apart from God and under human effort.

In somewhat less pretentious but equally real ways, we find ourselves trapped by the same kind of mind-set—a determination to forge our path through life without God or at least with a minimum of attention to Him. He seems too "otherworldly," too out of touch with our daily lives to really understand us. Moreover, He seems to want the kind of life that does more asking of us than giving to us, wanting love and service—in fact, wanting us to give up our life.

A passing tip of the hat here or there wouldn't be bad (especially if and when He does something nice for us, since we need to show appreciation for those moments) and even a little sacrifice now and then might not be a bad thing. But He never seems willing to settle for that. Give Him a finger, and He'll take the whole hand; give Him a hand, and He'll take an arm; give Him an arm, and He'll take us in our totality. No wonder we try to keep God at arm's length. You never know what He'll ask of us next if we get too close to Him, become too submissive to Him, offer ourselves to Him too completely.

We know all that in our more honest moments, but it is hard for us to see ourselves with the eye that reveals itself to us in our text. It is hard for us to hear this message as a word describing us. "Once you were alienated from God and were enemies in your minds." Yet if we are not for Him, we are against him. If we withhold ourselves from Him, we oppose His intention. If we keep Him at arm's length, we hold Him off altogether.

All of this is seen plainly by Paul as he describes in just a few words the need of the earth that brought the events of this night and tomorrow to pass. Through these events "now he has reconciled . . . by Christ's physical body through death" those who stood against Him, and now He calls them back to Himself. He has done all this "to present you holy in his sight, without blemish and free from accusation." He befriends and reconciles Himself to His enemies. He brushes aside our arm that is holding Him at bay and embraces us through the outstretched wings of the cross. He gives Himself in reconciling fashion to us who had made plain that we wanted nothing to do with Him. This is the marvel of His grace.

The Joining of Earth and Heaven

But His grace is far more than a mere theoretical statement. It is fleshed out in a body, acted out on a cross, empowered in human service, reconciled through blood. Here, if ever, we see how completely the Lord of all eternity has identified Himself with our human and earthly setting. Reconciliation between God and people, bearing dimensions and implications of an infinite sort, is effected by the Divine One from heaven through two poor earthly sticks of wood crossed over one another and holding fast the dying body of a human brother.

Is it, for that matter, much less of a wonder to look on this simple bread and wine before us this evening? Surely here, too, we can see nothing but the stuff of this earth.

Yet it was stuff of this earth just like this that Jesus took up in His hands on that first Maundy Thursday evening, saying such simple things as "This is my body" and "This is the new covenant in my blood," adding "Do this in remembrance of me."

"Remember Me time after time," Jesus tells them. For that is the implication of His statement. He is not simply saying, "Keep Me in mind when you eat bread and wine like this again in the future at other Passover meals." His command is much more far-reaching than that simple request.

He is saying that whenever bread and wine, the earthly substance that seems incapable in any way of bearing the presence of God to us, is coupled with His Word, He will be present for those who eat and drink. There He will be brought back among us in and through earthly things no more impressive than His body and blood once were to those around Him. The word He gives us will call Him back again in that special presence we call "sacramental" when we use with bread and wine the words He first spoke over similar substances.

This is the wonder among us this evening! The One in whom reconciliation was once worked out "by Christ's physical body through death" is present among us this evening and promises to feed us with His body and blood through this bread and wine. Can you ask for more? Can you live with less? When you want to know where He is, you are not to search the heavens; you are to direct your eyes here on earth and find Him in a body on a cross and present among His people in bread and wine.

Now, perhaps, comes what may appear the greatest wonder of all. When the world wants to find Him, you are the one in whom He is revealed. If God truly takes up the form of our world to make Himself known, then it follows that when He makes you His own in Baptism, strengthens and matures you with His Word, and feeds and nourishes you with His body and blood in the Sacrament, then He takes your poor mortal frame and turns it into a revelation of His presence.

The text plainly says that once God has worked His reconciliation among us through the earthly means of His Son on the cross, He has done it all "to present you holy in his sight, without blemish and free from accusation— if you continue in your faith, established and firm, not moved from the hope held out in the gospel. This is the gospel that you heard."

You can be "holy in his sight, without blemish and free from accusation," when your life is hidden in Christ. God is not asking you to do the impossible but rather to do what He has made possible. He tells you that you are to "continue in your faith," taking up the presence of Christ into your person and thus becoming His living, walking, talking presence wherever you go. You are asked only to confess that you have been caught up into Him who forgives sin so that you can represent Him as a servant represents the one who owns him/her.

When Paul urges you to be "established and firm, not moved from the hope held out in the gospel," He is using a picture taken from construction. It refers to foundational material. You are a person rooted deeply in eternity when you live in Christ, even though your life shoves up out of eternity into that history where God has placed you.

God calls you to be this earthly sign (in lieu of the flesh and blood of His Son and just as water, bread and wine sign His presence) wherever you are. Thus people will know that God is present. For He will make Himself known through you. Just give yourself to Him who has reconciled you. He will do the rest.

Good Friday

Passion Cross

Sermon Study

Text: John 19:17–18
Passion Reading: John 18:1–19:42
or John 19:17–30
(appointed Gospel)

Introduction: "Can Anyone Be Found?"

Martin Hengel, in his helpful book *Crucifixion,* gives an interesting passage from Seneca:

> *Can anyone be found who would prefer*
> *wasting away in pain dying limb by limb,*
> *or letting out his life drop by drop, rather*
> *than expiring once for all? Can any man be*
> *found willing to be fastened to the accursed*
> *tree, long sickly, already deformed, swelling*
> *with ugly weals on shoulders and chest, and*
> *drawing the breath of life amid long-drawn-*
> *out agony? He would have excuses for dying*
> *even before mounting the cross.*

(Martin Hengel, *Crucifixion* [Philadelphia: Fortress Press, 1977], 30)

"Can anyone be found" was a rhetorical question as far as Seneca was concerned. For pastors and laity preparing for Good Friday, it is no longer a rhetorical question but the occasion for a joyous "Yes, Jesus Christ was willing."

The agonies that He suffered, agonies that Seneca would have avoided by suicide, suggest the style of cross for this Good Friday's worship: the Passion Cross. Also called the Cross of Suffering, the Pointed Cross, and the Cross of Agony, it symbolizes the painful sufferings that Seneca described and Jesus endured. Occasionally it is depicted rising out of a chalice, suggesting Jesus' struggle with the cup of suffering in Gethsemane (John 18:11). That struggle resulted in His willingness to suffer, a desire for the cross of Passion.

Seneca found it inconceivable that a man would choose suffering. Melito is amazed that the one who was willing was God Himself:

> *He who hung the earth (in its place) hangs*
> *there, he who fixed the heavens is fixed there,*
> *he who made all things fast is made fast*
> *upon the tree, the Master has been insulted,*

God has been murdered, the King of Israel
has been slain by an Israelitish hand. O
stranger murder, stranger crime! The Master
has been treated in unseemly fashion, his
body naked, and not even deemed worthy of
a covering, that (his nakedness) might not
be seen. Therefore the lights (of heaven)
turned away, and the day darkened, that it
might hide him who was stripped upon the
cross. (quoted by Hengel, Crucifixion, p. 21)

Can any man be found willing? Yes. Thank God!

Background: The Conventional Wisdom on Passion

Jesus' contemporaries saw suffering as the direct consequence of sin and the Passion Cross as the place of deserved punishment. When the disciples passed a blind man on the road, they asked Jesus: "Rabbi, who sinned, this man or his parents, that he was born blind?" (9:2). The same idea of divine retribution in this life on the sins of an individual shows up in Luke 13:1–5:

Now there were some present at that time
who told Jesus about the Galileans whose
blood Pilate had mixed with their sacrifices.
Jesus answered, "Do you think that these
Galileans were worse sinners than all the
other Galileans because they suffered this
way? I tell you, no! But unless you repent,
you too will all perish. Or those eighteen
who died when the tower of Siloam fell on
them—do you think they were more guilty
than all the others living in Jerusalem? I tell
you, no! But unless you repent, you too will
all perish.

There is some Old Testament support for retributive suffering. Job 4:7 says "Who, being innocent, has ever perished?" (cf. also 22:4–5). To be sure, making individual suffering the mark of God's displeasure is not the whole counsel of the Old Testament. What's more, even the works-righteous Pharisees saw the idea break down when they found themselves suffering. But passion and guilt went together in the popular mind then, even as they do today. How many parishioners haven't asked you, "Pastor, why am I in the hospital? I've been good all my life." When someone suffered on an instrument as hated as the cross, then the conventional wisdom said, "He deserved it!"

Jesus' opponents thought that He was receiving the just reward for a sinful life and for His blasphemous claims to be God's Son. John's narration of the events of Good Friday contrasts Jesus' true innocence with the conviction of many Jews that He was guilty. After the betrayal, the Jewish officials and soldiers bind Him, and those cords must have remained until He had to carry His cross (John 18:12, 24). Taken first from the Mount of Olives to the house of Caiaphas, which probably was on the southwest side of the city, Jesus is struck by an official who thinks that His answer to Caiaphas is insolent (v. 22). Scenes like this don't happen unless someone is thought to be guilty.

The charges soon become explicit. Taking Jesus from Caiaphas to Pilate in the Antonia Fortress, the Jews say, "If he were not a criminal we would not have handed him over to you" (v. 30). Not only do they view Him as a criminal, but they believe that He deserves to die. He would have died already if the power of capital punishment had not been taken from the Sanhedrin. "We have no right to execute anyone" (v. 31). Jesus' innocence is heightened by Pilate's threefold declaration: "I find no basis for a charge against him" (18:38; 19:4, 6). The first two declarations infuriate the crowd, and the third brings a statement of Jesus' "crime:" "We have a law, and according to that law he must die, because he claimed to be the Son of God" (19:7). Is it any wonder that people mocked Jesus when He was finally hung on a cross? Only criminals were crucified, and like those hanging on either side, the one in the middle must certainly be guilty. His blasphemous claims put Him there. He deserved the Passion Cross.

Context: "Willing All This I Suffer"

He wanted it, too. He desired the cross not because He had any guilt, but for His exaltation. The language of John's gospel, the source of the Good Friday sermon text, shows Jesus' radically different viewpoint on the Passion of the cross. Even though paschō, the Greek word for "die" or "suffer," occurs 42 times in the New Testament, we do not find it in John's gospel. This evangelist prefers to speak of Christ's death with words like to be "glorified" or to be "lifted up." The usages are not euphemistic but intentional, presenting a whole different orientation to Passion. Both are present in John 12:23–33, a Passion prediction that we have not examined thus far in our series and a necessary context for the sermon text:

> *Jesus replied, "The hour has come for the Son of Man to be glorified. I tell you the truth, unless a kernel of wheat falls to the ground and dies, it remains only a single seed. But if it dies, it produces many seeds. The man who loves his life will lose it, while the man who hates his life in this world will keep it for eternal life. Whoever serves me must follow me; and where I am, my servant also will be. My Father will honor the one who serves me. Now my heart is troubled, and what shall I say? 'Father, save me from this hour'? No, it was for this very reason I came to this hour. Father, glorify your name!" Then a voice*

came from heaven, "I have glorified it, and
will glorify it again." The crowd that was
there and heard it said it had thundered; oth-
ers said an angel had spoken to him. Jesus
said, "This voice was for your benefit, not
mine. Now is the time for judgment on this
world; now the prince of this world will be
driven out. But I, when I am lifted up from
the earth, will draw all men to myself." He
said this to show the kind of death he was
going to die.

If Seneca asked the rhetorical question, "Can any man be found willing to
be fastened to the accursed tree?" Jesus puts a counter question to his
followers: "What shall I say? 'Father, save me from this hour?' No, it was for
this very reason I came to this hour. Father, glorify your name!" (vv. 27–
28). Jesus' willingness to endure the cross is heard later in Gethsemane:
"Shall I not drink the cup the Father has given me? (18:11b). The Father's
voice confirms Jesus' willingness: "I have glorified it, and will glorify it again"
(v. 28). The Father had glorified His name at Jesus' baptism and transfigu-
ration and now anticipates glorification at the cross, where Christ will "draw
all men to myself' (v. 32). We saw similar language in 3:14–16. Whereas
the world saw the cross as the place of deserved punishment, Jesus saw it
as His goal. There He would be glorified and draw all men to Himself and
the Father, bestowing eternal life. So we can approach the sermon text with
its straightforward description of Jesus' trip to Golgotha in the comfort that
our Savior went willingly.

A lamb alone bears willingly
Sin's crushing weight for sinners;
He carries guilt's enormity,
Dies shorn of all his honors.
He goes to slaughter, weak and faint,
Is led away with no complaint
His spotless life to offer.
He bears the stripes, the wrath, the lies,
The mockery, and yet replies,
"Willing all this I suffer." (LW 111:1)

Text: John 19:17–18

Carrying his own cross, he went out to the
place of the Skull (which in Aramaic is
called Golgotha). Here they crucified him,
and with him two others—one on each side
and Jesus in the middle.

This text is a simple description of a most monumental event. Other Johannine and Scriptural passages will help interpret the crucifixion, but the
simple, straightforward presentation should be carried into the sermon.

Verse 17a: Jesus is presented as actively going to His death. "Carrying his own cross, he went out." What Jesus probably carried on His shoulders was not the entire cross but the crossbeam, the patibulum.

Verse 17b: "He went out to the place of the Skull (which in Aramaic is called Golgotha)." John says that Jesus goes "out" because He goes beyond the city wall to Golgotha, which was probably the regular place for Jerusalem's crucifixions, just as in Rome the Esquiline Hill was the place for executions. Two modern sites are suggested for ancient Golgotha: the Church of the Holy Sepulchre west of the old city (and near the Lutheran Church of the Redeemer) and the Garden Tomb north of the old city. The latter site today has a rock formation that looks very much like a skull.

Verse 18a: "Here they crucified him." When the procession reached the place of execution, the normal practice was to nail the condemned man's hands to the patibulum. Note 20:27: "Then he said to Thomas, 'Put your finger here; see my hands." This horizontal beam was then fastened to a vertical beam. Sometimes the vertical beam had a small support for the feet, a suppedaneum, to which the feet were nailed. Archaeologists at Giv'at ha-Mivtar, one and a half miles north of the old city of Jerusalem, have discovered part of an olive wood cross with a seven-inch nail for the feet. The nail was driven first through a wooden block, then through the heel bones, and finally into the vertical beam.

Verse 18b: "two others—one on each side and Jesus in the middle." John keeps our attention on Jesus. That three people were crucified was not unusual, though the event was most hideous. What was unusual was the person in the center, who certainly was no criminal and was not even just an ordinary man. "The total obedience of Christ's total person, which he rendered to his heavenly Father even to the most ignominious death of the cross, is reckoned to us as righteousness. For neither the obedience nor the passion of the human nature alone, without the divine nature, could render satisfaction to the eternal and almighty God for the sins of all the world. Likewise, the deity alone, without the humanity, could not mediate between God and us" (FC SD iii 56).

Sermon Starters

Central Thought: Jesus went out and was crucified.

Outline 1: "Can Anyone Be Found?"
I. Introduction
   A. The event of Good Friday: the crucifixion
   B. The Passion Cross
II. The horrors of crucifixion
   A. Details
   B. Passion Cross also called Cross of Suffering, of Agony
   C. Seneca: "Can anyone be found?"
III. Yes, Jesus!
   A. Exposition of the text

B. Why He endured the Passion Cross:
  1. For our sin, not His
  2. For our eternal life (cf. 3:15)
  3. For His exaltation (cf. 12:32)
IV. Wonder before the Passion Cross
  A. The Passion Cross evokes wonder.
  B. Melito's lament
  C. Your future meditations on the cross
V. Conclusion: Jesus was found!

Outline 2:   **"Willing All This I Suffer"**
  I. Introduction
    A. We worship because "A Lamb Alone Bears Willingly" (*LW* 111).
    B. Brief exposition of the text
  II. Uncomplaining!
    A. Today, we view the Passion Cross, the Cross of Suffering, the Cross of Agony.
    B. The horrors of crucifixion
    C. Then why does Jesus "bear willingly"?
  III. "Willing All This I Suffer"
    A. For our sin, not His
    B. For our eternal life (3:15)
    C. To draw us to Him (12:32)
  IV. Conclusion: What wondrous love!
    A. Jesus' Passion Cross calls for our devotion.
    B. "Oh wondrous love!" (*LW* 111:3)

Outline 3:   **"O Strange Murder, Strange Crime!"**
  I. Introduction
    A. The Passion Cross
    B. As you look at Golgotha, marvel at who is on the middle cross of suffering.
  II. Jesus, true God and true Man!
    A. The cross is a place of terrible suffering for a normal man.
    B. Jesus, the God-man, endures the Passion Cross.
    C. Melito's lament
  III. Why submit to this "strange murder, strange crime"?
    A. The God-man dies for our sins, not His.
    B. He suffers for our life.
    C. The Passion Cross is to draw us to Him.
  IV. Conclusion: How much God loves you!

Sermon: The Passion Cross

John 19:17–18

It is hard to find words adequate to an occasion like Good Friday. Of course, it is hard to find words adequate to death even in a general way. You surely have noticed how hard it is to speak with people who have recently suffered the loss of a family member or a dear friend. What do you say? What can you say that fully and adequately addresses the occasion? We all know the usual words of comfort, the invitation to "let me know if there is anything I can do." But even when we have said the very best things we know to say, there is that strange empty feeling that we carry away—a sense that we have not really said anything that made sense, that really touched the depths of the grieving one.

It is very, very difficult to find words adequate to address death. Yet somehow we must speak. For there is no way to ignore death. And inasmuch as all of life points to death, somehow we must deal with it as though it were the capstone of life, the end to which all life is lived.

The Awe-fullness of Death

What a bitter thing that makes out of life, some may say. Should life not be lived to its fullest, almost in defiance of death? Granted that death will come, but why live in its shadows? Let it find us, but let us not seek it. With words and thoughts like these we often seek to avoid the pain that death inflicts on us.

And there is at least this measure of truth in such thinking: We should not dwell morbidly on death and thus darken the days of our living. Nor should we seek death, as though suicidal wishes were in any way healthy.

But the greater truth to which we point is the very simple fact that we are all dying people. And there is something mysterious about death that helps us understand an equal mystery about life. There is an awesomeness about our grave that gives us reason to consider our life more seriously than if we ignore our end in favor of a frivolous waste of the life that leads up to that end.

Every sickness and ailment that incapacitates us is a sign of our dying. When the powers that we assume in responsible living are taken away or are seen to be deteriorating, a small glimpse is given into our death. For if one thing must be said about death, it is simply this: In that moment our body's fullest weakness is exposed. There all the presumed powers of life are seen for what they are—failing and finite. There is no time when we are more helpless than in the moment when our breath fails our body and it lies completely in the care and keeping of those still living. This is the ultimate humiliation (and it is, indeed, a humiliation) of death, that we are now completely "at the disposal," so to speak, of others. Our power is drained. Our strength is gone. Our body depends on another's final care. And it returns to the dust from which it came.

Death is, therefore, a most awe-full thing in the sense that one must be filled with awe at the power it exerts over the best of our powers. And it is, if possible, even more chilling to our bones to think of another person exerting his or her living powers over our living powers to drain our life away from us. When one hears of a murder or even a prolonged torture that one person inflicts on another, our heart cries out in terror. How dare someone bring death or even the awful premonition of death through torture on another living person? Our hearts quaver when we hear of such events.

How much the more, then, must we not be filled with awe when we hear of a person who submits to the torture of fellow humans, inviting death, as it were, to be inflicted on Him? This is not a suicidal person but One who stands between the powers of evil and the powers of good. We refer, of course, to the Person who holds front and center of this day's attention, Jesus Christ. If death is such a monstrous horror to begin with, and if the terror of death is magnified when one person visits torture and/ or death on another against that person's will, then surely we must stand in awe of this Jesus of Nazareth, who stands before His accusers without defending Himself against death.

The Awe-fullness of Christ's Death in Particular

This death commands our attention on this day of days. For it is the day around which our faith rises or falls. It is the day on which our very life hinges.

The One whom we watch—even more particularly, the One whom we judge along with Herod and Pilate and all sinners!—is the One "by whom all things were made," "the Word made flesh" (John 1). That is the great mystery of this moment, that the Creator of life must now give up His life. This would be a terrible moment under any circumstances if an ordinary and good man were to be on trial and judged worthy of death contrary to all decent justice. But to know who walks this way of sorrows, to know that this Man who, "carrying his own cross, went out to the place of the skull (which in Aramaic is called Golgotha)," is none other than the One by whom "all things were created: things in heaven and on earth, visible and invisible" and in whom "all things hold together" (Col. 1:16–17)—to know this is truly to be filled with awe.

It is to this dreadful understanding that the Passion Cross points us. With its pointed edges, often made, in fact, out of nails, the cross (also called the Cross of Suffering, the Pointed Cross, or the Cross of Agony) symbolizes the painful sufferings that Jesus, Son of Man and Son of God, endured. Sometimes it is pictured as rising out of a chalice, suggesting Jesus' struggle with what He called His cup of suffering. Only hours before His crucifixion, after Peter had tried to defend Him in the Garden of Gethsemane, Jesus admonished Peter to put away his sword, saying, "Shall I not drink the cup the Father has given me?" (John 18:11).

This suffering of God's Son becomes our hope and our salvation, of course. And this fact makes the awe of this moment still greater. For the Lord of life now places Himself into the position where either the Lord of death will overcome Him or else He will, Himself, take the measure of the lord of death and assume the title of Lord of life and death. If one too quickly insists that He was lord of death before the crucifixion, one has not reckoned fully with the powers of darkness, who had long ago turned life into death and made themselves at least would-be lords of death. This, after all, is one of the primary ways the cross is described—as the battleground where all this would be threshed out.

It is this that causes us to stand almost wordless before the cross. What can one say here? How can one describe what is happening in this event? To simply say, "Here they crucified him, and with him two others—one on each side and Jesus in the middle," seems hardly adequate. And yet that is what the writer says, for in this moment there seems so little else to say. How simply yet how deeply this statement points us to the moment of all moments.

Here, as it were, the Lord of life lays bare His breast to the worst that the powers of darkness can do. Those who would beat on the Lord's creation must now beat on the Lord of creation. He confronts them openly in a life-and-death setting. It is as though He were saying to the demonic forces, "What you do in humiliating My children in their living and in their dying, do now to Me. Do not spare Me, for if you can overcome Me, your pretentious lordship exercised so long over My creation is truly yours forever. But now, in this moment, I stand squarely between what you do to My children and your worst intentions. 'This is your hour—when darkness reigns' " (Luke 22:53)

What is there to say in this hour? What is there for us to do? We stand on the one side of Jesus and the evil ones beat on Him from the other side. If they can break through Him, they have us fully in their power. And we have no resistance to them without this One. Nor do we have power to help this One being crucified.

The Passion Cross is now planted firmly in the ground. We can only stand and watch and hold our eyes and mouths wide open with awe and wonder. We can only hope and trust.

The Glory of the Lord Revealed in Jesus' Dying

It is interesting to note that the Greek word for "die" or "suffer," pascho, which you can recognize from phrases like "paschal lamb" sometimes applied to Jesus, occurs 42 times in the New Testament. But John, the writer of our text, never once uses the word. Instead, he refers to the mission and task of Jesus with phrases like "lifted up" or "glorified."

That is how we read of Jesus' prediction that He would be crucified in Jerusalem, telling His disciples, "The hour has come for the Son of Man to be glorified" (John 12:23). In the closing prayer of the long discourse that Jesus gives to his disciples at the Last Supper, He prays, "Father, the time has come. Glorify your Son, that your Son may glorify you. For you granted him authority over all people that he might give eternal life to all those you have given him" (17:1–2).

In words like these we see into the depths of that simple account that reads, "Here they crucified him." Here on this cross we have a window into the very heart of God—that heart into which we journeyed through the text on the last Wednesday of this Lenten season. Through this cross we catch a glimpse of how very deeply God's love is rooted—so deeply that it holds fast the Passion Cross.

It took much to hold it fast. We are not the only ones who stand by and watch helplessly, as it were, while the cross takes its toll of suffering on this Crucified One. Are we not joined silently by the Father, who also watches? Can you not see the tears in His eyes and the torrent of anguish that floods His own heart as He stands by and hears His Son cry out, "My God, my God, why have you forsaken me?" Can you not feel His temptation to pull the cross out of the ground, to free His Son from those nails, to swallow up in one mighty gulp of judgment a world that would do such a thing? Do you not see the Father's grief in the Son's suffering? He has Himself commissioned His Son to the task. And the Father's name is glorified in the Son's obedience, the obedience He sought from us all but found only in Him. Is not the Father tempted to relieve His Son whom He sent and to let the curse of the oppressors break through to us?

But He stands there as silently as we do. And He does nothing, as though He were as helpless as we. Here, if ever, you see the love of God laid bare—on the cross of Jesus' Passion. Here the "glory of the Lord" is most fully revealed.

Our Dying in Order to Live

"Don't you know that all of us who were baptized into Christ Jesus were baptized into his death? We were therefore buried with him through baptism into death," St. Paul tells us (Rom. 6:3–4). In these words Paul addresses us with the realization that the death on which we have been reflecting is our death. Christ's death for you has become the stuff of your death. Your baptism tied you to this moment on which your attention is focused through the text in such a fashion that His death to sin became your death to sin. Although you still feel its deathly pull, when it beats on you unmercifully, there is One who steps between as your Defender. It can still threaten you terribly, but One who has fought death and overcome it can place His hand over death's mouth and silence its threats when the crucial hour comes.

You feel its miserable pull in hundreds of little deaths every day, of course. They are all signs of the ultimate death that will one day visit you. These little deaths may be the tortures of people who taunt you, belittle you, and tear you down. They may be your own failures, the embarrassments and humiliations you endure as you move through life, trying so hard to be one thing while really being quite something other. They may be the illnesses and ailments that remind you of your journey to the grave. You die many ways every day.

These little deaths terrorize you, but associating yourself with this cross is a very freeing thing. The death that would ultimately destroy you has already beaten here on your Lord, and it did not overcome Him. You, who feel the pummeling of life, live in Him whom the pummeling could not destroy. You even feel the dying that He endures as you go your way to your grave. But you also know even now that powerful Word that raised Him from the grave and that joins you to Him.

Therefore, live as though your life were a rehearsal for death with a litany of dying—dying to the world, dying to sin, dying to evil, dying to yourself. You are, as it were, daily writing the obituary of your life, the last word of which cannot be known until your death. What has been written up to now can be nailed to this cross if it is not what you want your life to be about. But what remains to be written can be written with the life that comes from this cross—a living in Him, whose death and resurrection is your hope and salvation.

Words do indeed fail us in the face of death—even Jesus' death. But His death is about life. And there is much to say about living when it is in Him.

The Resurrection of Our Lord

Glory Cross—Victory

Sermon Study

Text: *Colossians 3:1–4*

Introduction

Think about next Monday, the day after Easter! Midweek Lenten services are over. Holy Week is over. Easter's special services are over. And you hope there are no funerals, critical illnesses, or pressing counseling sessions. The prospect of much-needed rest in the future helps shape your actions and attitudes as the busy Lenten season reaches its joyous climax.

Life-styles are like that. Some guiding thought shapes daily conduct. In West Side Story it was being a Jet. "When you're a Jet, you're a Jet all the way, from your first cigarette to your last dying day." During the Viet Nam era, "Yippies" had their own code of behavior that affected their conduct and dress—and everybody else's as well. Now some of them have become "Yuppies," young urban professionals, and like Preppies, they even have their own published handbook. By the time this book gets into your hands, social commentators probably will have identified many other life-styles.

Your proclamation to the saints this Easter Sunday is about the guiding principle that informs the Christian life-style. Our attitudes and actions are all caught up with the risen Christ. Right now that means that our life is hidden with God in Christ and so, not seeing glory, we set our hearts on the glorious Christ at the right hand of God. In the future, Christ our life and glory will be fully revealed. That's what guides our present—not unlike the prospect of Easter rest giving you the extra energy for Holy Week.

The Cross of Glory symbolizes all this quite well. The splendid rays of the sun are seen behind the cross, but the sun itself is not visible. So our glorious future is now hidden with Christ, who was crucified on Good Friday. His Easter resurrection, the rising of the Son, sends us the hope of glory. All of that affects life-style, yours and your hearers'.

Background: "You Can Have It All!"

The Colossians were being tempted to "have it all." Much like the modern American woman, who is lured by television commercials to pursue a career (top management, of course), family, and social life with no thought about reality (Does she ever sleep? Do laundry? Get crabby?), the Colossians were being led on by false teachers to think they could have it all: Christ, glory, religious ritual, humility, satisfied desires, and whatever else happened to be in vogue.

The allurements of the heretics laid a heavy stress on wisdom, as attractive then as it is to many today. This wisdom seems to have been an early form of the Gnosticism that matured in later centuries. In our preparations for Maundy Thursday we saw this wisdom manifest itself as cosmic preoccupation, people gazing into the hidden things of eternity and overlooking the incarnate Redeemer. This same wisdom showed itself in regulations about life-style, our concern now as we prepare for Easter Sunday.

There were all sorts of "how-to's" with the heretics' style of life. Religious ritual was very important, an emphasis that must have appealed to the congregation's Jewish members. There were rules about eating and drinking, religious festivals, New Moon celebrations, and Sabbath observance (Col. 2:16). Asceticism was practiced, to a point at least (v. 21; cf. v. 23). Humility was in vogue (v. 18). And so was Christ.

That's what made it so appealing. All the how-to's of this life-style were not intended to replace Christ. The heretics just wanted to supplement the Gospel; they wanted to add the insights of other religions. That made it all so appealing. You can have it all—Christ, too.

Epaphras knew that this syncretism was deadly, but he must have felt stymied in his efforts to combat it. So he sought help from the learned apostle. Paul was very impressed by Epaphras's pastoral concern. "He is always wrestling in prayer for you, that you may stand firm in all the will of God, mature and fully assured. I vouch for him that he is working hard for you" (4:12–13). With that commendation of Epaphras, Paul took up the problem of the seductive, you-can-have-it-all life-style and called the Colossians back to the cross and "Christ in you, the hope of glory" (1:27).

Context: Christ's Glory Alone

Paul says, "You can't have it all, and what's more, you don't want it all!" Your life-style depends either on Christ or on "human tradition and the basic principles of this world" (2:8).

The latter, says Paul, is futile. Epaphras apparently told Paul about improper conduct by members of the congregation, because Paul attacks the moral bankruptcy of the heresy. "They lack any value in restraining sensual indulgence" (2:23). In 3:5–11 he catalogs some sins that the heresy must have fostered: anger, rage, malice, slander, filty language, lies, and prejudice. A more significant list is in 3:5: "sexual immorality, impurity, lust, evil desires and greed, which is idolatry." That last word, "idolatry," pinpoints the real problem. Your attitudes and actions are either based on Jesus Christ or they are based on something else. It's a matter of the first commandment. "See to it that no one takes you captive through hollow and deceptive philosophy, which depends on human tradition and the basic principles of this world rather than on Christ" (2:8).

Paul doesn't ask the Colossians to choose. They already have. "So, then, just as you received Christ Jesus as Lord, continue to live in him, rooted and built up in him, strengthened in the faith as you were taught" (2:6). In order to reassure his readers that Christ is indeed the only basis for our attitudes and actions, Paul writes about the glories of Christ. Whereas the false teachers delight in the worship of angels (2:18), Christ is more: "He is the image of the invisible God, the firstborn over all creation. For by him all things were created: things in heaven and on earth, visible and invisible, whether thrones or powers or rulers or authorities; all things were created by him and for him. He is before all things" (1:15–17). Christ is not static; His glories are seen at the cross, where He proved His preeminence. "Having disarmed the powers and authorities, he made a public spectacle of them, triumphing over them by the cross" (2:15). Note well: The worldly philosophy that the heretics promote says that the crucified One, the suffering One is the disarmed spectacle. That's why crucifixions were on thoroughfares. Paul exalted that the crucified Christ made a public spectacle of them all. He upsets the appealing wisdom and fine arguments of the world.

At the cross legalism lost its power over daily life because Christ forgave our sins. "He forgave us all our sins, having canceled the written code, with its regulations, that was against us and stood opposed to us; he took it away, nailing it to the cross" (vv. 13–14). The forgiven Colossians participate in the cross and resurrection by their baptism (v. 12), are rescued from the dominion of darkness (which the world considers glory!), and are in the kingdom of light (1:13). This is the kingdom of Christ's resplendent glory, and Christ, for the Colossians and for us, is the hope of glory (1:27).

The Christian life-style should flow from that cross of glory. Questions of attitude and action are to be answered Christologically, not legally. "Therefore do not let anyone judge you by what you eat or drink, or with regard to a religious festival, a New Moon celebration or a Sabbath day. These are a shadow of the things that were to come; the reality, however, is found in Christ" (2:16–17). That conclusion, "therefore," leads Paul into detail on some nuts and bolts issues of daily living in the practical section of the letter. But before doing that, he offers a general principle for Christian living. That is our text.

Text: Colossians 3:1–4

Since, then, you have been raised with Christ,
set your hearts on things above, where Christ
is seated at the right hand of God. Set your
minds on things above, not on earthly
things. For you died, and your life is now
hidden with Christ in God. When Christ, who
is your life, appears, then you also will ap-
pear with him in glory.

One approach to studying this text is the sequence past, present, future. Paul addresses those who have been baptized, people already incorporated into the death and resurrection of Christ. This makes the present a time for Christians to pursue a life-style filled with Christian qualities, a marked contrast to the unregenerate life. When Christ returns, the glory of this life will be fully manifest, but for now it is hidden with Christ in God.

Verse 1a: "Since." Because the letter is addressed to "the holy and faithful brothers in Christ," *ei* here is best translated "since," not "if" as in the AV.

Thus the following exhortations are based on the fact that the Colossians are already incorporated into Christ. That is, the Gospel here precedes the third use of the Law.

"Raised with Christ" is explained by 2:12: "having been buried with him in baptism and raised with him through your faith in the power of God." See 3:3: "For you died." See also Romans 6:4–5. The death, burial, and resurrection of Christ are historical events in which the Christian shares because of Baptism. "With Christ" is difficult for the western mind but true, nonetheless.

Verses 1b–2: "Set your hearts on things above. . . . Set your minds on things above, not on earthly things." The Greek word *zēteite* is usually translated by the English imperative "seek." The NIV rendering, "set your hearts," reminds us that the Christian has a yearning for the higher things. Seeking is not just an intellectual activity. Cf. the use of *phronein* in Philippians 2:2, 5. Herodotus I.94; Sophocles; and Oedipus the King, 659, give precedents for the NIV's "set your hearts." The pursuit of "things above" with heart and mind should be contrasted to the unregenerates' studious pursuit of earthly things (Phil. 3:19; Rom. 1:25). Cf. Matthew 6:33: "Seek first his kingdom and his righteousness."

The objects of daily pursuit are the "things above," not "earthly things." Earthly things are defined in 2:8: "hollow and deceptive philosophy, which depends on human tradition and the basic principles of this world rather than on Christ." Symptoms of this philosophy are listed in 2:21–23 (regulations of outward conduct) and 3:5–10 (specific sins). Because "you died with Christ to the basic principles of this world" (2:20), seek the "things above, where Christ is seated at the right hand of God." The things above are daily life with God, a life often hidden to earthly sight (3:3) but traced in Christian virtues (vv. 9–14). The "things above" are not to be equated with heaven, nor is "above" spatial. That is determined by the clause "where Christ is seated at the right hand of God," about which the Lutheran Confessions speak:

> *The right hand of God . . . is not a specific*
> *place in heaven, as the Sacramentarians*
> *maintain without proof from the Holy Scrip-*
> *tures. The right hand of God is precisely the*
> *almighty power of God which fills heaven*
> *and earth, in which Christ has been installed*
> *according to his humanity in deed and in*
> *truth without any blending or equalization*
> *of the two natures in their essence and essen-*
> *tial properties. (FC SD viii 28)*

Verses 3–4a: "Your life is now hidden with Christ in God. When Christ, who is your life. . . ." On Christ as our life, see John 14:6; 1 John 5:12; Phil. 1:21. The full dimensions of the Christian life are not known by the unregenerate, whose approach to life is dominated by externals such as possessions, regulations, rituals, etc. Even the Christian is unable to grasp all the glories of life in Christ. "Dear friends, now we are children of God, and what we will be has not yet been made known. But we know that when he appears, we shall be like him, for we shall see him as he is" (1 John 3:2; cf. Rom. 8:18). This is wonderful Gospel with which we can encourage our hearers not to evaluate their lives solely on the basis of what they see and judge. It reassures them that they can expect a full and glorious revelation on the day when Christ, our life, is no longer hidden.

Verse 4: "When Christ ... appears, then you also will appear with him in glory." God's glory, that is, the splendors of His divine being, will be revealed at the return of Christ. The Old Testament speaks of glory in relation to God (e.g., Ex. 34:29), and the New Testament applies it also to Christ (1 Peter 4:11). The present text looks to the future revelation of divine glory and says that Christians will also share in that glory because of their participation in the body of Christ. The coming glorification of believers is well attested by Scripture. "Those who are wise will shine like the brightness of the heavens, and those who lead many to righteousness, like the stars forever and ever" (Dan. 12:3). "Glory, honor, and peace for everyone who does good" (Rom. 2:10). "If we are children, then we are ... coheirs with Christ, if indeed we share in his sufferings in order that we may also share in his glory" (8:17; cf. also 1 Peter 1:7). This glory of the believers with Christ will be visible to sight (Is. 35:2), but for now it is hidden with Christ in God, an object of hope: "Christ in you, the hope of glory" (Col. 1:27).

Here this Sunday's cross, the Cross of Glory, is most apt. The glories of Christ's resurrection stream from behind His Good Friday cross. That is the occasion of the worship celebration. But for the believers, baptized into the body of Christ, the glory is still obscured by the crosses of their own lives. Their lives are now hidden with Christ in God but will be revealed fully in glory at the end of time. Thus the glories of the Easter celebration are a plea to "set your minds on things above" until the full revelation of glory.

Sermon Starters

Central thought: Our attitudes and actions are shaped by the risen Christ.

Outline 1:   **The Cross of Glory**
  I. Introduction: Does Easter make a difference? Let's look at your life-style.
 II. Can you have it all—Christ, too?
     A. Today's alluring life-styles
     B. The Colossian heresy, a syncretism with Christ
III. No! It's Christ or this world
     A. Epaphras's concern
     B. Paul's advice:
         1. Life not based on Christ is futile.
         2. Your life is with Christ by Baptism.
         3. Any rays of glory come from the cross.
IV. Your Easter life-style

A. Identity: You are part of the risen Christ.

B. Activity: You seek things above.

C. Hope: You look forward to the revelation of glory now hidden with Christ in God.

V. Conclusion: Crosses and rays of glory

Outline 2: **Handbook for Easter Living**

I. Introduction: The Cross of Glory

A. The sun rises behind the cross.

B. The glorious resurrection illumines our life.

II. Life-style handbooks

A. Preppies, Yuppies, and other groups have handbooks on their unique life-styles.

B. Colossians 3:1–4 is your handbook for resurrection living.

III. "You have been raised with Christ."

A. You are not of this world.

B. Note the Colossian heresy.

C. You are Christ's.

1. You are buried with Him in Baptism.

2. You are alive in His resurrection.

IV. Your handbook for resurrection living

A. His resurrection illumines your daily life.

B. Seek the things that are above.

C. Know that your life is hidden with Christ in God.

D. Anticipate your appearance with Him in glory.

V. Conclusion: On with resurrection living!

Outline 3: **A Hidden Holiday**

I. Introduction: The attraction of Easter

A. For Christians: Our Lord is alive.

B. Those who have not been to the cross cannot penetrate our joy today at the tomb.

II. A hidden holiday

A. "Your life is now hidden with Christ in God."

B. It is hidden by burial at Baptism.

C. It is hidden with His resurrection.

D. It is hidden with His glorious ascension.

III. Celebrating the hidden holiday

A. "Set your hearts on things above where Christ is."

B. Anticipate that "you also will appear with him in glory."

IV. The Cross of Glory

A. The glorious sun is behind the cross.

B. Our Easter life is hidden with Christ in God.

Sermon: The Cross of Glory—Victory

Colossians 3:1–4

Easter is like something hidden and then found.

It is like an egg put into a secret place and discovered by a child after all the eggs were thought to have been found.

It is like a gift deposited under the pillow of a loved one to be discovered just at the moment of disappointment, when it seemed that the birthday had been overlooked or forgotten.

It is a God-given gift wrapped in such a way that nobody recognizes it as a gift until it is unwrapped and suddenly revealed to be of priceless worth.

Easter is like that—a grand and glorious surprise!

The Hiddenness of Christ

Jesus was like that. Nobody had really understood with whom they had walked and talked through the years of His ministry. His words had certainly borne deep wisdom. He had certainly taught with authority. His deeds had been mighty. His life had been extraordinary. He lived with and conveyed remarkable peace that impressed people. He had a sense of being that people had not encountered in anybody else.

Yet through this extraordinary life something was hidden within Him. Peter, who confessed Him to be the Messiah, the Son of the living God, had not really uncovered what was hidden within Jesus. Even Mary, who had borne Him and raised Him, remained mystified by the strange quality in Jesus that set Him apart from others.

But if there had been mystery in His living, it was only magnified in His dying. That day must have dispelled any lingering notion that in this package of human flesh God had hidden any kind of special gift. How could a death-wrapped man contain a gift from God? If the cradle was hard to comprehend, the cross was even harder. If God had intended to make a gift of Jesus, His intentions were surely bent out of shape by human deeds that reduced the intended gift to a mere mortal, death-bound human, subject to life's grotesque twists and turns.

Surely any thought that God had wrapped a gift in the flesh of Jesus had to be laid aside at the cross. The mysterious hiddenness that lay like a shadow over Him throughout His life was most deeply in effect on that day when the powers of darkness swallowed Him into the cavern toward which all humans are bound—the cavern of death. For three days that hiddenness was total.

The Revelation of Christ

It is unfortunate for us, in some ways, that we know already on Good Friday what will happen three days later. We prepare for the Easter meal and lay out our Easter clothing already during the days of this dreadful hiddenness in the grave as though one just naturally can expect Jesus to be raised from the dead.

That is very deceitful, for it keeps us from a full realization of the dreadful awfulness of Good Friday and Holy Saturday as it was experienced by the disciples and friends of Jesus. For them, the days after the crucifixion were not spent in anticipation and preparation. They were days of darkness in which the presence of the Lord they thought they had discerned in Jesus of Nazareth lay most deeply hidden, and they themselves went into hiding lest they be caught in the dragnet of those who had crucified Jesus.

We who stand on this side of the resurrection, that great event we celebrate today, can hardly imagine how dark those three days were for the disciples and friends of Jesus.

But the stark contrast between their hopelessness and despair in the days after Good Friday and the glorious wonder of the angelic question, "Why do you seek the living among the dead?" marks the joy of this Easter Day. Only when you know clearly that this Man is dead and you never again expect to see Him on earth again, does your heart jump with the singular joy of Easter when He reappears from the grave. Only when you have heard the mournful words of those who had taken His body down from the cross, prepared it all too hastily for its burial, and borrowed a tomb in which to lay the body can you catch some idea of the emotions of this day, when He suddenly appears alive again to Mary Magdalene, to Peter, to men on the road to Emmaus, and to the Eleven gathered behind locked doors. For these people there had been no expectation of Easter, even though Jesus had told them that it would happen. They had not understood His announcement before His crucifixion, and it sounded even more absurd after it. They just sat numbed and bewildered without the faintest idea of what might happen next.

Into such a state of affairs Jesus reappeared. Suddenly He is walking and talking with the two on the way to Emmaus, asking about the events that seemed to have disturbed them so much, as though He were a curious inquisitor. Then He becomes an interpreter. He comes to people filled with fear and brings peace into their midst. He speaks as though they should have taken it for granted that He would return. He had told them He would, had He not? Could they not trust His Word just as He trusted His Father's Word, by which He could go into death and return again? The Father could be trusted to keep His Word. Jesus was the living proof of that as He rejoined them from the dead.

This incomprehensible turn of events, this turnaround from sorrow to joy, from death to life, gave them new eyes with which to see Jesus and a new heart with which to receive the gift that had now been fully revealed. What had been hidden within Jesus was now more clearly seen—or at least something of what He had brought into the world with His presence and His life and His death could now be better sensed. Although many implications remained up in the air, it was clear that someone who could enter the realm of death and return was in touch with powers and authority and understandings that none before Him had ever been able to claim. Surely something special and different and unique had happened. A Man who had not been devastated by death was present. Where death had been beaten back, people had to sit up and listen.

It was plain to them that in Christ God had been present among them— hidden, to be sure, but working something out among them that they had never quite seen or realized. He was the specially chosen One, in whose life and death everything about life had been rearranged. If death no longer had the last say on earth, one's whole assessment of how the heavens and the earth function had to change.

Our New Life in Christ, Crucified and Raised

Today's text says this very thing: "Since, then, you have been raised with Christ, set your hearts on things above, where Christ is seated at the right hand of God" (Col. 3:1). Through Christ's resurrection, we get a brand new view of things. When we are joined to His resurrection, as Paul says we are in our baptism, we gain a new perspective and a new power for living. Everything that once seemed true is now overthrown for a new truth.

Put it this way: Through the resurrection you see the future in terms of life, where once it all seemed to point to death. If God brought Jesus back from the dead, then you can be sure that He will also bring you through the darkness of death into the same kind of resurrection when you hide yourself under the wings of Christ. Death remains a monster among us, to be sure, but it has no last or ultimate word to say to us, for "your life is now hidden with Christ in God," Paul tells us (v. 3). Death cannot intimidate you when your life is invigorated with the powers that are stronger than death. When "your life is now hidden with Christ in God," the powers that protected Him in death also protect you.

Think of what that means! The One who is more powerful than death is surely also more powerful than all the arrows that fly toward you daily, threatening to put you into the grave. He who acted in the hour of Jesus' death and raised Him again on the third day can and does act equally as strongly over against lesser things than death. If your very life is "hidden in Christ," then surely your life here on earth is protected against everything that threatens you by the same God who will see you through death just as He saw His own Son through death. That is quite a promise! And you can bank on it as surely as you see the resurrected Christ on this day standing free of the grave.

This, of course, changes everything for you in almost every way imaginable. To be hidden and raised with Christ means that you can "set your hearts on things above, where Christ is seated at the right hand of God." You can "set your minds on things above, not on earthly things. For you died, and your life is now hidden with Christ in God." We still need the things of this earth, in other words, to sustain our life here, but they all look different and have a different value when we have been raised with Christ in Baptism. Being joined to Christ makes it possible to set our hearts on "things above."

This phrase does not suggest some kind of voice or vision come from

God or a specially pious life devoted to some special spirituality raising you above earthly things. It means that you can now see your earthly possessions and surroundings with eyes that are focused through new lenses. You realize that these things cannot give or take away your life. The One who raises Jesus from the dead is the One who governs the life and death issues. The things on which you depend so much here on earth are transient—part of the death-bound surroundings that are momentarily significant in the sense that they come from God as a gift to you for temporary care. But they are not able to see you through the ultimate mysteries of life when death must be taken into your body and you become "hidden in Christ."

In the previous chapter Paul wrote that you were "buried with [Christ] in baptism and raised with him through your faith in the power of God, who raised him from the dead" (2:12). This is all wrapped up in that simple little phrase, "your life is now hidden with Christ in God." Just as the resurrection is such a marvel only when it is seen against the apparent finality of His death, so also your new life in Christ seems so incredible precisely because you seem so bound to sin, so locked into death, so inescapably confined to this earth in your thinking and your living and your daily needs.

The Hiddenness of Our Life in Christ

It is hard to grasp this wonder, is it not? You seem to be so much like you always were, even though you are "hidden in Christ."

It is as though you were a gift wrapped by God in an almost unrecognizable package that, when fully opened, is the sign and token of His presence among us. We said that about the Christ in the beginning, and now we must speak of ourselves as such a gift. When God hides your life in Christ in Baptism, He leaves it wrapped in that virtually unrecognizable package of your flesh, beset as it is with sin and weakness and death.

What we shall be in the resurrection has not yet appeared. What we want to be as we set our hearts on "things above" is by no means yet realized, and we seem so bound to the things that are below. What our victory will be when Christ who is our life appears seems at present to be nothing more than a series of defeats as we sin daily, lose strength in our body, and journey unfailingly to the grave. What we presently experience is so far from what we want to be or hope to be that we would despair were it not for a simple promise: "When Christ, who is your life, appears, then you also will appear with him in glory" (v. 4).

Easter, then, is a call to faith in the God who fulfilled His promise to raise Jesus Christ from the dead and who promises in the same way to raise us from the dead also when the time comes.

But Easter is much more. It is a call to new life in Christ right now. This new life is symbolized by the Cross of Glory that stands before you on this Easter morning. The splendid rays of the sun are seen behind the cross but the sun itself is not visible. In like fashion, your glorious future is now hidden with Christ, who was crucified and is now risen.

We receive a glimpse of that glorious future in its early coming. The rays flow from the still-unseen sun to rise behind the cross. The resurrection of Christ is your promise that you not only will be raised on the last day but that already now you are raised with Him as you are joined to Him in your baptism and by the faith in which you now live. Your present life, hidden in Him, glows with the glory that is yet to be revealed in its fullness, for it is surrounded by the glory of the Lord that first dawned on the world in the resurrection of Christ.

The resurrection stirred up a ferment that keeps life happening in the very midst of death. Where death keeps laying claim to the earth in general and to your life in particular, you can confront those destroying powers with the cross into which you were baptized and hold them at bay with it. A power is offered you from that cross emptied of its burden and from the Risen One, who was once fastened to that cross, enlivening your present existence.

Just as you are "hidden in Christ," Christ is hidden in you in this life-giving moment. The Risen One in whom your life is hidden shines out through your life like rays of the sun rising behind the cross as the promise of what will one day be revealed fully. Through faith your life, still so deeply encrusted with the appearances and weaknesses and troubles and sins of this world, is given over to Christ. You are hidden in Him, and He becomes hidden in you. Just as what happened to Him in His death and resurrection became yours in your baptism, by the same baptism your life was taken up into Him, and He hid within you to make your life His very own.

That is why we say that Easter is like something hidden and then found. It is God's life hidden in Christ, revealed fully in the resurrection, and found in us through our baptism.

In other words, Easter is like God unwrapping a package that nobody really recognized as a gift until He unwrapped it, revealing it in that moment to be the greatest of all gifts we could hope for. It is like God unwrapping your life and showing it, in turn, as the hiding place of Christ, who guards you from the powers that would destroy you in life and death and who then empowers your life to go forth in His name.

Easter is new life—Christ's life in which you hide and your life within which the new life of Christ hides.

Easter is Christ breaking open the tomb of your life and raising you to new vision, new hope, new deed, new life.

Easter is the gift of an open tomb—and a living Christ—and a new you.